HALIFAX
& CALDER VALLEY
MEMORIES

The publishers would like to thank the following companies for their support in the production of this book

Main Sponsor
Marshalls plc

Artisan Fireplaces
Briggs Priestley
Halifax Borough Market
R. Collett & Sons
Crossley Heath School
Joseph Dobson & Sons
RP Dowsland Electricians
Fan Systems Group
Freudenberg Nonwovens LP
Finn Gledhill
Hartley & Sugden
HBOS
McVitie's Cake Company
Nestlé Confectionery
Nethercoats
Parkinson-Spencer Refractories
Rice-Jones
RSA Group
Southdale Homes
Suma
Thornber Chicks Ltd
Woolshops

First published in Great Britain by True North Books Limited
Britannia Works, Halifax, England. HX3 6AE
01422 344344

ISBN 1 903204 93 3

Text, design and origination by True North Books
Printed and bound by The Amadeus Press

HALIFAX
& CALDER VALLEY
MEMORIES

CONTENTS

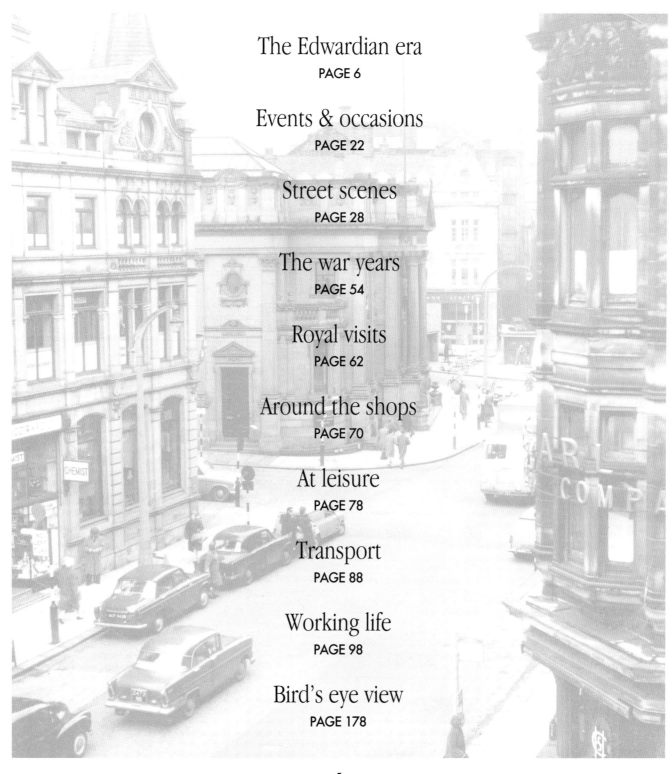

INTRODUCTION

'Halifax & Calder Valley Memories' is an opportunity to indulge in time travel. There is no magical Tardis to transport you back through history. What we have is page after page of nostalgia. Wonderful images, all carefully captioned with informative and witty text, will help the readers return to the last century without ever leaving the armchair in which they are sitting. As you turn each leaf you will be able to share those days when dad was a lad or grandma was a flapper. Our towns and boroughs have changed so much since their times that it is hard to bring to mind just how everything used to be. Thank

goodness for the camera. Without a pictorial record so much of our recent history would be a mere memory. You will have personal experience of some of the scenes, while others will be brought to mind by the stories our parents and grandparents told us. In this book you will be able to see what it was they were talking about when referring to certain streets and events. There are other photographs and memory joggers that you will be able to remember for yourself. Perhaps this book might even settle a wager or two.

Halifax is now a town of over 80,000 inhabitants, though that rises to nearly 200,000 when considering Calderdale as a whole. There was no reference to Halifax in the Domesday Book, but a parish church has stood here since the middle of the 12th century. Halifax had a fearsome reputation for strict law enforcement and the Gibbet Law of Halifax can be traced back as far as 1280. The Gibbet (pictured above) was believed to have first been put in place to deter cattle thieves, but was later used to deter and punish cloth stealers. The Lord of the Manor of Halifax had the power to try and execute any felon for thefts of the value of 13$^{1/2}$ pence and upward. The origin of the town's name provokes some discussion. Some believe that it developed from 'holy face', referring to the legend that John the Baptist's head was buried here after his execution. Others have it that the name is a corruption of 'holy flax (field)' or simply 'hay field'. The coat of arms of Halifax includes some of the elements from that of the Earls Warenne, who held the town during Norman times. However, this was just a small hamlet and even by the 14th century there were only 20 households here. They were mainly involved in the woollen trade, a sign of things to come as textiles would be the lifeblood during the industrial revolution. This initial cottage industry developed during the 15th century to the extent that over 500 homes were built in the neighbourhood at this time. Its steady increase in importance as a textile manufacturing base was reflected in the building of the magnificent 18th century cloth centre, the Piece Hall. With great strides being made in mechanisation and the building of new mills during the late 18th and early 19th centuries, people flocked from the land and into the town to take up employment in the rapidly expanding industry. Between 1801 and 1851, the population almost trebled, rising from below 9,000 to over 25,000. In the next 50 years it was to double again.

It is from this time onwards that 'Halifax & Calder Valley Memories' bases much of its focus. Rediscover the way we shopped, how we played, the jobs we had and the styles of transport we used to get around. They will all hold something special for each and every one of us delving into the pages of this book.

Calderdale has much to be proud of and a number of its best known and longest established firms have allowed us to access their internal archives. This has enabled us to recount the history of these companies from humble beginnings, in most cases, to leading positions in their chosen area of expertise. These organisations have tremendous social, as well as commercial significance, as between them they represent the places of employment for many thousands of Halifax and Calder Valley people. We are very grateful to the directors of these businesses for their co-operation and valuable support. We all love looking back on times when the pace was slower and the manners more genteel. It is time to turn that first page and indulge ourselves in a wave of nostalgia.

TEXT	ANDREW MITCHELL, STEVE AINSWORTH
PHOTOGRAPH COMPILATION	TONY LAX
DESIGNER	SEAMUS MOLLOY
BUSINESS DEVELOPMENT EDITOR	PETER PREST

THE EDWARDIAN ERA

A UNIQUE SELECTION OF LOCAL IMAGES FROM A PERIOD AROUND 100 YEARS AGO

Halifax's handsome Town Hall, from Corn Market, can be picked out from almost anywhere in town. The spire reaches high above the surrounding buildings and makes a fine landmark as well as reference point. When Halifax was incorporated as a borough in 1848, the early administrative offices were scattered all over the town. It made sense to get them all under one roof, though it took five years before any real plans to create a corporate centre were given consideration. In the end a trio of designs were submitted by as many interested parties. The Council, Edward Akroyd and John Crossley all had their own ideas and supported conflicting views. As no final decision could be taken or agreement made, Charles Barry, the architect of the Houses of Parliament, was asked to come and judge the submissions. Just to complicate matters further, or possibly seeing an opportunity, the great man turned his nose up at all three proposals. He was then invited to put forward a plan of his own. This was duly carried out and accepted. The foundation stone was laid in 1861, but Barry had died the previous year and the work was completed by his son, Edward Middleton Barry. The huge tower and spire are decorated from top to bottom, where a quartet of seven foot, stone angels stands guard.

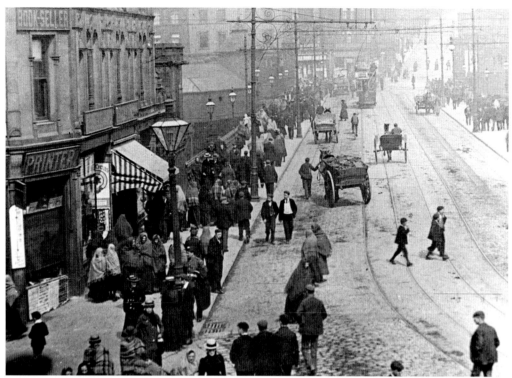

expectancy of only 45 at best. In the other photograph, the chimneys of Crossley's carpet mills and other similar enterprises stand out clearly. The Grand Theatre, on the right, dated from 1889. Designed by Frank Matcham, it was opened by Wilson Barrett. The latter, an actor manager and playwright, was one of the most respected figures on the London stage in those days, so it was quite a coup to get him to Halifax. Barrett had a particular flair for melodrama, a form of theatre much loved by the Victorians. The Grand replaced the Gaiety Theatre that burned down in 1888 and became a popular repertory theatre. In the early 1940s it was used as a cinema, before returning to its former usage after the war. It was knocked down in 1957 after part of the ceiling collapsed and the building was declared unsafe.

Above and below: There will not be a reader of this book who can recall Halifax's North Bridge as it looked in the early 1900s, but although some of the buildings have gone, others still remain and the bridge itself continues to serve its purpose of providing a link over the valley from one side of the town to the other. This photographs takes us back in time when horses and carts dominated the streets, but they had started to take care when confronted by the new wonder of public transport, the electric tram. Very soon, further advances in travel would see automobiles moving along Northgate in greater numbers. The old cobbled setts were littered with horse droppings. An idea of the poverty of the time that was experienced by many can be gleaned from looking closely at one group of women on the left, wrapped up in shawls to keep out the cold. The gaunt faces suggest that life for them was hard. Their children often died young, struggling to combat the ravages of measles, whooping cough and scarlet fever. A baby born in those days had a life

Top right: The Edwardians loved the freedom that the electric tram gave them, enabling the general public to get access to transport at the end of their street, rather than having to make the journey to the train station. The latter was fine for longer journeys, but the facility of being able to nip

into Halifax or Hebden Bridge at short notice was something that they only dreamed about in Victorian times. This tram ran on the Cow Green to Hebden Bridge route and was one of the first electric cars to be used. The open top for the passengers afforded a grand view across the rolling countryside, but that was very much for the romantics when the rains came. Pragmatists travelled on the lower deck. Seen in Mytholmroyd in the early 1900s, we can only pity the poor driver. His open cab must have been a dreadful place when the wind blew, the rains fell and the temperature plummeted. He needed more than a mugful of Van Houten's cocoa to revive him. The Dutch company, Holland's equivalent of Fry or Cadbury, could claim many things about its products, but resuscitation was not one of them! It came as something of a relief to everyone, passengers and drivers alike, when later generations of trams were fully enclosed.

Right: If you wanted to get around town at the turn of the 20th century, then a stout pair of shoes was required. There were no motorbuses, no electric tram and definitely no motorcars on the roads. There might be the odd bicycle, but in general, if you wished to get anywhere, then it was Shanks's pony for you. Looking down Crown Street from its junction with Waterhouse Street, we can see that it was quite a pull up from Corn Market. If you did not fancy walking around the town, then you could hire a horse drawn cab and perhaps take in a visit to some of the prestigious shops in the vicinity, such as R Whiteley's hatters or Melia's and Lipton's stores.

Below and right: Elland Town Hall was built in 1887 and cost £7,000. It opened for business in 1888, but was never actually used as a centre for civic affairs. Over time it has seen use as a public hall, snooker club, cinema and bingo hall. It is a Grade II listed building that was badly damaged in a fire in November, 1994. Elland had its own gaol house (right) at one time. Situated opposite the Town Hall, it looked, from the outside that is, to be quite a pleasant looking building. However, the regime within those walls was less appealing. Elland Silver Band practised there on occasion in the past. However, the building fell into disuse when the new police station opened on Burley Street and was deployed as a bus shelter for a while. It was demolished in 1963, along with the ghosts of the miscreants who were once incarcerated there.

was the contestant achieving the longest knock over an agreed number of hits, or by the average knock. The game is thought to have its origins in medieval times and was often played on Shrove Tuesday and Good Friday. But it may be older still: its name derives from the Norse for ball game – 'nurspel' suggesting that it may have arrived with the Vikings, though 'spell' is also a dialect word for a piece of wood. Interest in the game reached its height in the 19th century. Though it retains its enthusiast even today, interest dwindled as men became able to afford other sports such as golf. Soon after this photo was taken Todmorden Golf Club was formed at Todmorden Edge on the uplands overlooking Centre Vale Park. Land was obtained from three farmers at Flailcroft and Dyke Farms, consisting of 34 acres (acquired at a price of 7s. 6d (37.5 p). per acre), in addition to two cottages for use as a clubhouse and as a home for a professional. The nine hole course opened on 4 May, 1895.

Below: Among the earliest depictions of the game of knur and spell is this one featuring a match which took place near Rive Rocks above Todmorden around 1890. Matches played on the tops often attracted large crowds of spectators. The game was played between two or more contestants, commonly a local expert and a leading player from another town. The winner

Below: Crossley's Mill and the workers' houses provided the backdrop for the 1900 Hebden Bridge Agricultural Show held at Calder Holmes. It was both a chance for local farmers to show off their best breeds and for traders to mount displays that might encourage the notoriously careful landowners to part with their cash on some new machinery. There was talk that a petrol driven contraption called a tractor was under development, but the farming community thought little of the idea, safe in the knowledge that the horse and plough would do them for many years to come. Families whose associations were with factories and not farms had a great day out, enjoying seeing the animals at close quarters. The children loved the side shows, the sheepdog demonstrations and the noise of the crowd and looked forward to another wonderful time the following year.

Right: James Street is just off Huddersfield Road, Elland. This group of happy chappies was off on a jolly boys' day out. They were certainly riding in style, on board a specially converted charabanc. It is a good job that the health and safety officials were not around in their day or a Stop notice would be plastered all over the 'charrer'. Packed in like so many sardines in a tin, they were probably held in more tightly than any safety harness could achieve. With a toot of the horn, the four and twenty men set off on a journey that surely must have included the odd watering station at some hostelry on the way. It would not have been a proper day out otherwise. There seems to be a sort of social pecking order with regard to the seating arrangements. Those on the back seat appear to be better dressed, at least better hatted, than those in front of them. The coach belonged to the John Harling transport company. Harling delivered steel plates for Dempster's Rose Mount Iron Works and used a lorry to transport the goods. When weekend came, this enterprising company slotted a charabanc body in place and it was ready to take passengers off to the seaside.

Above: After the 1870 Education Act, it was compulsory for all children between the ages of 5 and 13 to attend school, although it is unclear how many of them were able to do so regularly. In winter in the countryside many children faced a teeth-chattering walk to school of several miles. A large number simply did not turn up because of this or because their parents needed them to do jobs that brought in extra cash, despite the constraints of the law. Lessons lasted from 9am to 5pm, with a two hour lunch break. Because classes were so large, pupils all had to do the same thing at the same time. The teacher barked a command and the children all opened their books as they were told. At the second command they began copying sentences from the blackboard. Lessons concentrated on the three Rs and children gained much of their knowledge by reciting things parrot fashion, until they were word perfect. There was no messing about, because the cane was a useful tool for gaining obedience. They may not have been the happiest days of their young lives, but these kiddies left school proficient in the basic subjects.

Above: The bobby in the centre foreground had better be careful. If the tramcar is heading his way, that authoritative pose of standing to attention might have to be disturbed. Two young women are having an earnest conversation by the church gate as a group of boater-hatted men talk over important events of the day. To their right we have several lads sporting knickerbockers or plus fours. The elderly lady at the bottom left might well have been a widow, dressed as she is in black. The whole scene shouts of the early years of the 20th century, when the horse rather than horsepower was still very important. The photograph was taken at King Cross, outside the former Church of St Paul. This separate parish was created in 1846. Until then King Cross was part of the Halifax parish. The church was built in 1847 at a cost of nearly £5,000, including the fittings and furniture. It had room for 450 worshippers, but the King Cross population had risen to 17,000 by the end of the century. There was little room to extend, so a new one was built on Queen's Road. The last service was held at the old church in 1912. By 1930 the building was unsafe and it was largely demolished, leaving just the tower and spire that still stand there today inside a small park created in 1973.

Left: Heptonstall was an important village in the days before the canals, railways and steam power had their effect on settlements and industries lower down in the valleys. It was formerly a centre for hand-loom weaving and the cottage windows, designed to maximise the amount of light coming in, are a reminder of the days when weavers worked at home. Heptonstall had a cloth hall, at which the finished work was traded, even before Halifax had its Piece Hall. Mr Holt, the grandfather of the late local historian Jack Uttley, is the adult seen on Towngate. Beyond him, The Cross Inn awaited its first drinkers of the day. It is thought to date from the 17th century and that would not be surprising, because little seems to have changed in the village for several hundred years. Clinging to the hillside above Hebden Bridge, Heptonstall has been referred to as Haworth without the Brontes, which is a little unfair. After all, it does have its own literary connections. Sylvia Plath, the American poet and wife of the former poet laureate, Ted Hughes of Mytholmroyd, is buried in the churchyard. This troubled woman committed suicide in 1963 and an inscription on her headstone reads 'Even amidst fierce flames the golden lotus can be planted'.

Below: Down by the River Calder, the 1914 Mytholmroyd Charity Demonstration Day was held. It was inaugurated in 1903 and was, by now, well established. The event was staged every year until 1939. The tradition was revived in 1960 as

Mytholmroyd Gala. Since then, it has been a source of summertime fun for everybody in the district, with fancy dress competitions, fairground rides, charity stalls, brass bands and traditional games. Unfortunately, in recent times volunteers to organise the event have become thinner on the ground and it would be a shame if such an occasion with a rich heritage was lost to the local community. Back in the early years of the last century, the annual procession and show soon became one of Mytholmroyd's highlights of the year. It raised money for good causes, as we can tell from the actions of the fireman on the right as he holds out his collection box. The person under the umbrella used it as a parasol because the long shadows suggest that they had a lovely day on which to parade. Traders were quick to spot an opportunity for a bit of advertising. The poster on the wall extolled the virtues of the furnisher Hanson and Son. According to the advert, this establishment could furnish your house from top to bottom.

Below: Wards End, at the junction with Commercial Street and Fountains Street, has been home to the grandiose Victoria building for over a century. It has been the premier centre for entertainment for local residents ever since its inception. The foundation stone was laid in 1899 by Alderman GF Smith, following a procession to the site that was witnessed by a crowd of thousands. Victoria Hall, as it then was, took its name in honour of the monarch who died shortly before it opened its doors to the paying public in 1901. Manchester's Halle Orchestra provided the entertainment and began with the National Anthem, followed by the funeral march from Beethoven's Third Symphony, to mark the Queen's passing. It was to become the largest dance and theatre centre in Halifax, but by the end of the 1950s was becoming distinctly tatty and careworn. It was sold to the Corporation in 1960 and underwent a major facelift that took over 18 months from May 1962. Readers who enjoyed their visits to the 'Vic' might recall the diverse entertainment that was provided there half a century ago. Local pop star Don Lang

(Gordon Langhorn), famous for his 'Auctioneer' and 'Witchdoctor' hit records, was just one attraction, while wrestler Big Daddy (Shirley Crabtree) also performed in his home town. The photograph dates from the early 1900s and the hall is now known as the Victoria Theatre.

Right: This specially posed photograph was taken on a locomotive that was part of the Blake Dean Railway. High up in the valley slopes above Hebden Bridge, we can still find the remnants of a once mighty enterprise. Several stone pillars stand in the Hebden river, relics of the trestle bridge that carried the railway that was used to assist in the building of the Walshaw Dean moorland reservoirs. The bridge became unstable and was demolished in 1912, but that was after it had carried the line used to transport navvies and materials up from the valley floor in order to complete the work. Many of the workforce lived in huts in a shanty town near Heptonstall, nicknamed Dawson City. This family group on the steam engine would not have gone near

the rough men building the reservoirs because, as demonstrated by the smart clothing, it was so obviously a social class or more above such people. The railway started from Whitehall Nook at Heptonstall and ran around the top of the hill at Widdop Gate. From there it crossed the valley via the trestle bridge, ending at the site of the reservoirs five miles away. Hebden Bridge architect WC Cockcroft designed the remarkable structure and such was his confidence in his work that he was in the first truck that crossed the bridge on 24 May, 1901.

Above: Five people - four passengers and the conductor - were killed when this tram went out of control in Sowerby Bridge. The picture show stunned onlookers at the scene in Bolton Brow in the wet October of 1907. Over forty people were injured in the accident which was caused by problems with the vehicles braking system.

Above: Pictured standing at the doorway of 15 Bank Street, in Todmorden, is Richard Stansfield, then aged 57. With him is his second wife, Sarah, alongside his four daughters from his first marriage – Ellen, on the far left holding the baby, together with Mary, Patience and Sarah. The back-to back house at Bank Street (the other side was Goshen Terrace) would be the Stansfield family home for the next two generations. Back-to-back housing was a pragmatic approach to the acute housing shortage of the latter half of the 19th century. The ever increasing population of the North's industrial towns and cities led to more and more folk being crammed into smaller and smaller spaces. Tens of thousands of speculative, often jerrybuilt, back-to-back houses were constructed. On hilly sites the back-to-back element was also part of an up-and-over building scheme, with 'under dwellings a common feature as well as landing-access only. Most were demolished in slum clearances in the 1960s. Around the time this picture was taken, Richard Stansfield was employed as a mechanic fitter for Jeremiah Jackson's textile engineers in Todmorden. Richard's son James Stansfield was also a mechanic fitter for the same firm having earlier began his career as an apprentice loom-maker for Fielden Bros. Harry and Richard Stansfield, Richard's grandsons, would also follow careers with Jeremiah Jackson's. In 1946 Harry Stansfield became managing director of the firm. Richard Stansfield died in 1908 at the age of 65, not a bad innings for the times.

Below: King George V and Queen Mary passed though Elland on their way from Halifax to Huddersfield on 11 July, 1912. It may have been just a fleeting visit, but the townspeople were not going to let the occasion pass by without displaying their sense of national pride and fidelity to the monarchy. Streets were decked out in glorious fashion, perhaps with bunting saved from the coronation celebrations the year before. People dressed up for the occasion, fishing out their Sunday best. The large lady on the right wore the same frock that she done the previous year, but the working classes did not have an extensive wardrobe and the dress would not be worn all that often and it had to last. The children scrubbed up well and looked very smart in all their finery. This would probably be their only chance of seeing this king and queen in the flesh and it was important that they looked their best. New Street had previously won a prize as being the best decorated street in Elland. It pulled out all the stops to repeat its victory and the effort was worthwhile when it retained its title. At the end of the day, the streamers and flags came down and were put away until they were needed again. That day would come in different circumstances when they marked Armistice Day in 1918.

Left: Looking down the Dewsbury Road into Elland, with Coppera's Farm on the left, we can see that the journey up this slope must have been a nightmare for the poor horse that was dragging its cart along what was little more than a muddy track for most of the year. When it rained, the surface turned into an oozy mess and in winter the snow and ice combined to make it impassable on occasions. In the early 20th century, not all main roads had yet been given a decent surface and movement around the hillier parts of the region was difficult, to say the least. Those living in the more remote farmsteads and hamlets cursed the weather, especially during the severe winters that we often had. They could be cut off for many days at a time and there were no such things as helicopters to conduct a rescue or make a food drop if things got too bad. It was a case of grin and bear it. People had to be sensible and stockpile certain provisions to be ready for such an emergency. Those with animals to tend found it the hardest as the sheep had to be fed and, at times, rescued. Working in the countryside was not a job for the fainthearted. Those who talk about the good old days need to be reminded of the privations that many endured.

Below: The Royal Family was held in the greatest of esteem in the days before we started to question the monarchy's role. Perhaps the rot set in during the abdication crisis of 1936, but our present Queen is dearly loved. Back in 1911, the people of Hebden Bridge asked no such questions. For them, and indeed the rest of the nation, the King was someone to be honoured, respected and cherished as our head of state. On 22 June, George V was crowned in Westminster Abbey during ceremonies that lasted some seven hours. One of the most touching moments came when his son, the Prince of Wales, knelt at his feet promising allegiance and service. Little did his father know that this was the man who would bring the monarchy into crisis a quarter of a century later. In Hebden Bridge there was no crystal ball and so they celebrated the present. A grand Coronation Arch was erected at the junction of New Road and Bridge Gate and everywhere there were garlands, flags and streamers. The King's father, Edward VIII, had died the year before and the traditional period of mourning observed. Now it was time to look forward and raise three cheers for King George and Queen Mary.

Edwardian Age was a time of wonders. The world was changing at an exciting and remarkable pace: motorcars, bicycles, aeroplanes had all just recently made their appearance. Electric lighting and telephones were a novelty still to be wondered at. And yet here, in a tiny corner of Calderdale is something of a wonder, a reminder of an age already past: a water wheel. A century earlier the many valley's cutting through our hills must have been littered with water wheels, millponds and small factories. Many of their remains can still be seen, though often hidden and overgrown. By 1900 however water wheels had, in mainstream – no pun intended – industry, been succeeded by steam engines decades earlier. But here one survives. And in seemingly good order. The wheel was turned by water taken from a pond at a higher elevation. The wooden shute bringing the water to the wheel can clearly be seen. Once set in motion the water wheel would, via a series of linkages, drive any machinery. Above and to the left of the water wheel can be seen part of the gear wheels which would take power into the building.

Above: Although modernised and remodelled, quite a few of the premises in the Woolshops have retained their former lines. If you look closely at these buildings today, there is still some part of the area that has kept its soul and has not completely sold it to the developer. The newspaper billboards make interesting reading. One tells of a diamond haul in a raid on a mail van and another promises an exposé of Rudolph Valentino's love life. Nothing new there, then. Our newspapers today would also include a mixture of crime and sexual titillation. We have not altered much in our interests and dubious moral values in the 80 years since one photographer pointed his lens down the lane. The modern Woolshops Shopping Centre opened in 1983, keeping the named link with activity in this part of town that was so central to its Victorian economy. The original shops were more like warehouses where the woolstaplers or dealers held their stocks.

Right: One of the most rare and unusual photographs recording life as it once was in the upper Calder Valley is this one taken at Holme House Mill at Booth in the early years of the 20th century. The date is somewhere in that Golden Age between the death of Queen Victoria in 1901 and the outbreak of the first world war in 1914. The

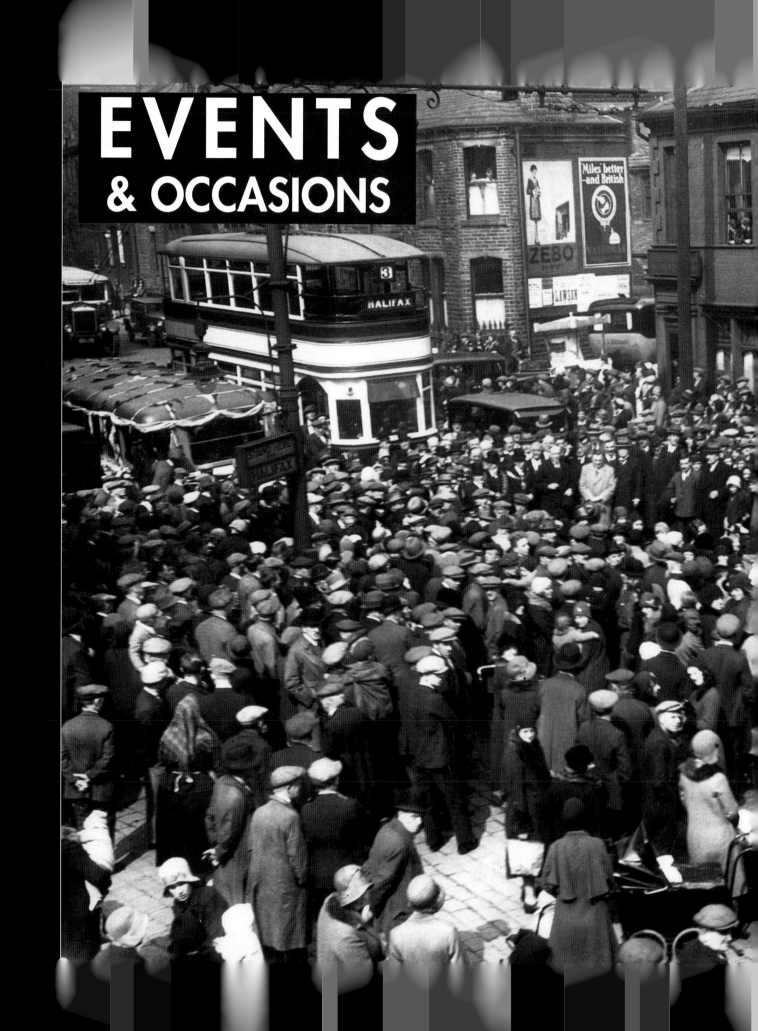

EVENTS
& OCCASIONS

Left: In many parts of the country trams were still running through town centres after the last war and into the 1950s. However, they came to an earlier demise in Brighouse. The last one ran from Briggate into Halifax as long ago as 1931. The occasion attracted a large number of onlookers as local dignitaries made up the passenger list on that final journey. It was the end of a fairly short era as the life of the service was only about 30 years in length. But, in the last century everything started to move at a much quicker rate than had been seen before. There were massive changes in healthcare, industry, technology and transport. During the short life of the Brighouse tram we had a world war, the introduction of motor cars, the first aeroplanes, electricity on our streets and in our homes, radio transmission and life saving drugs and medicines being developed. Those saying goodbye to the tram wondered what might come along next. Rather perversely, public transport was something that would alter little over the rest of the century. We had buses then and we have them now. Although steam locomotives have gone, the railways still function much as they used to. In some towns and cities, such as Sheffield and Manchester, the tram has returned and that aspect of public transport seems to have turned full circle.

Below: Brighouse and Halifax were both represented by their mayors when the bus service between the towns was inaugurated in 1931. Boldly sporting their chains of office, they took centre stage among the other Corporation officials and transport representatives as the new service was christened. The very first bus in the Calderdale area ran from Parkinson Lane via Pellon to Mount Tabor in Halifax. This route was commenced in 1912 and was served by a single deck vehicle. The Great War meant that attention was focused on the war effort and only a small number of buses were deployed to augment the tramway. No substantial increase in the bus fleet took place until 1925 when 12 Dennis 50 cwt models were purchased. Tramcars continued to be built in the 1920s, with a total of 27 new ones being produced in the Halifax Corporation workshops. But, the writing was on the wall when, in 1929, the service from Brighouse to Bailiff Bridge was withdrawn. In that same year, Halifax introduced its first double deck motorbuses and from then on the takeover gathered pace. By 1932, there was a fleet of 90 and the tramlines started to disappear. By the end of the decade they would be gone forever.

Right: In the days before the NHS raising money for hospitals was a serious concern. Here is a scene from one of the many Hospital Charities Galas held at the Lane Head recreation ground. Taken in the mid-1930s the Brighouse School of Dancing's children's section is being carried on a flat bed truck belonging to Walshaw Drake & Co of Rosemary Dyeworks in Brighouse. The lorry was not state of the art even in those days, and with its solid tyres must have provided a very uncomfortable ride for the young dancers. The girls on the

HERE COME THE CONQUERING HEROES

R.L. CUP WINNERS 190 1921 1939

float have taken ancient Greece as their theme. On either side of the float can be seen the words 'Beauty is truth' and 'Truth is Beauty'. Written in 1819, 'Ode on a Grecian Urn' was the third of the five 'great odes' written that year by Keats, including - Psyche, Melancholy, and Autumn. Grecian Urn is not one of the 'great odes' but it contains the most discussed two lines in all of Keats's poetry – 'Beauty is truth, truth beauty, – that is all/Ye know on earth, and all ye need to know.' Whether or not these young ladies had ever heard of Keats, or if they had been forced to memorise his famous lines at school, we will never know. Though if most youngsters' attitude to poetry is anything to go by it would not have mattered much to them. Greek themes however were very fashionable during the 1930s as part of a general and international interest in health and fitness.

Left: The crowd at Odsal Stadium for the 1939 Challenge Cup semi final between Halifax and Leeds was the highest ever recorded in Britain for a rugby league match. Stated here as 66,308, it is reported in Bradford Northern's (now Bulls') records as being only 64,453. Perhaps we have to take the figures with a pinch of salt because the match was played on All Fools' Day, but what is not in question is the commitment of both sides. The goal was the trip to Wembley and an opportunity for supporters to stroll down the Way into the magnificent stadium a month later. Halifax won the day in front of this large crowd and went on to meet Salford. Odsal was a relatively new ground, having been bought by Northern as a former quarry and tip site in 1933. The site was transformed and the first game held there on 1 September, 1934. Halifax played at Odsal again in front of an even larger crowd when another new record attendance of 102,569 fans came to see the Challenge Cup Final replay with Warrington in 1954.

Above: Halifax Rugby League Football Club was founded in 1873 and became a founder member of the Northern Rugby Union in 1895. Based at Thrum Hall, this would be its home until 1998 when the ground was sold to Asda for use as a superstore. Proudly holding the Challenge Cup aloft, the players from the successful 1939 team deserved the adulation of the crowds that cheered them on the open topped bus ride around the town centre. Halifax had beaten Salford 20-3 in front of over 55,000 at Wembley on 6 May. This was, until then, the largest ever Cup Final crowd. Only the soccer equivalent attracted more. Larger attendances were recorded after the war, but for this number of supporters to travel to London from Lancashire and Yorkshire was, at the time, quite remarkable. Wages were low and travel difficult, but both Salford and Halifax supporters did their clubs proud in making the trip to the twin towers. Northerners first descended on the famous stadium in 1929 when Wigan beat Dewsbury and, despite the distance from the part of the country where the game was centred, Wembley has been the Cup Final venue for the vast majority of matches ever since. A programme for the 1939 game cost just sixpence (2.5p), but can be found on eBay for the princely sum of £125.

COPYRIGHT C. HWood

Above: A sunny and ceremonial Saturday afternoon in Halifax in May, 1952. This photograph taken, at the bottom of George Square looking down Commercial Street, shows the Territorial Army Band under the leadership of Bandmaster F Ashton Jones. The band formed part of the 250th anniversary parade of the Duke of Wellington's Regiment which marked the beginning of two days of celebrations. The huge crowds which turned out for the event can be seen on the photograph with one man climbing onto the roof of Gledhill Hosiery shop, right side of the picture. The stack of the old Odeon cinema can be seen in the distance, centre right, and the Yorkshire Penny Bank building is in front. The parade of shops on the right of the shot included Asquith's umbrella and handbag shop, and Ainley's tobacconist who sported a sign advertising State Express 555 cigarettes.

Below left: Mayor Dr Stella Brown presenting Coronation mugs to pupils at Roomfield School, Todmorden, in this photo from May, 1953. Mugs and other memorabilia of the Coronation of Queen Elizabeth II are an indelible recollection of anyone at school at this time. The mugs became instant heirlooms getting pride of place in display cabinets in homes across the land. Queen Elizabeth's father had died in early 1952, the actually coronation in Westminster Abbey not taking place until 2 June the following year. For many youngsters the event was memorable not for the acquisition of commemorative mugs, but for their first sight of television. The status of television would be given an enormous boost by the announcement that the actual Coronation would be broadcast live on by the BBC.

Above right: It may not be as grand or as prestigious as Harrogate's Great Yorkshire Show, but the annual agricultural show held on Savile Park is one that Halifax residents have looked forward to every summer since World War II. Although most of us are 'townies', we do love to see country pursuits brought to our doorstep. The grand marquees with their displays of country crafts, flowers, vegetables and home made produce are always full of interested visitors. The parade rings for the large animals and the demonstrations of bee keeping and shepherding bring young and old together as they gaze fondly at the sights before them. On the far side of the parkland, budding showjumpers ride their mounts over double oxers and gates designed to catch a careless fetlock or two. Trade stands advertise their goods and services and there is a smell of beef and fried onions in the air. Tractors rumble across grass and dogs can be heard barking in the distance. The merry chatter of people, enjoying a day out from behind their TVs and computer consoles, drifts across the air. Children guess the name of the doll in the hope of winning her. Others estimate the number of Smarties in a jar. Occasionally a message about a lost kiddie comes across the tannoy, but all we need is for the sun to shine and it will be what everyone wanted, a great day out.

STREET SCENES

This group of photographs, taken from just about the same spot over a period of nearly 100 years, shows The Cross at Elland from the Southgate corner. The oldest picture was taken before the bank, seen in the other photographs, was built in 1894. Scallywags and the Bodega Bar had replaced Swale's by 22 April, 1981, and in this scene we can tell that the oak tree, just a thin sapling over 40 years before, was

maturing quite nicely. The iron railings around the church have been replaced by a neat hedge. They would have been melted down and reconstituted as some form of weaponry in the 1940s as part of the war effort. In the view of the Church of St Mary the Virgin that dates from the first months of the Second World War, it seems as if a funeral is taking place. T Swale also had a corn mill on Westgate in addition to his shop here. This part of town

got its name from the simple wooden cross that stood on the site where the church was built. St Mary's was formerly a daughter of the parish church of Halifax and can trace its history back to 1180. The tower has a peel of eight bells, well known as one of the best in the area. The old Norman bellcote, the small stone turret on the ridge of the roof, used to house the Sanctus bell.

The tramline was something akin to that of a horizontal switchback ride as it snaked its way through George's Square in 1930. There is a trio of little lads standing dangerously on the tracks, involved in some deep conversation, so let us hope that they nipped out of the way before the next tram came along. In truth, the boys were fairly safe as the clanking of the trams was warning enough for even the hardest of hearing. The boys were probably from middle class families, if their clothes are anything to go by. The knickerbockers, Eton style collars and smart jackets suggest that their parents were not short of the readies. The cloth cap worn by the boy on the right did not necessarily suggest someone from a lower class as this type of headgear crossed social divides for the younger generation. It was as he grew older that boaters, homburgs, trilbies or bowlers would start to put him apart from the cloth cap brigade. This was an era when people were still very class conscious. The working classes even had an inverted sense of snobbery, not wanting to be seen to adopt middle class values. Unfortunately, these working classes became the unemployed classes as the decade unfolded and the depression years kicked in with a vengeance.

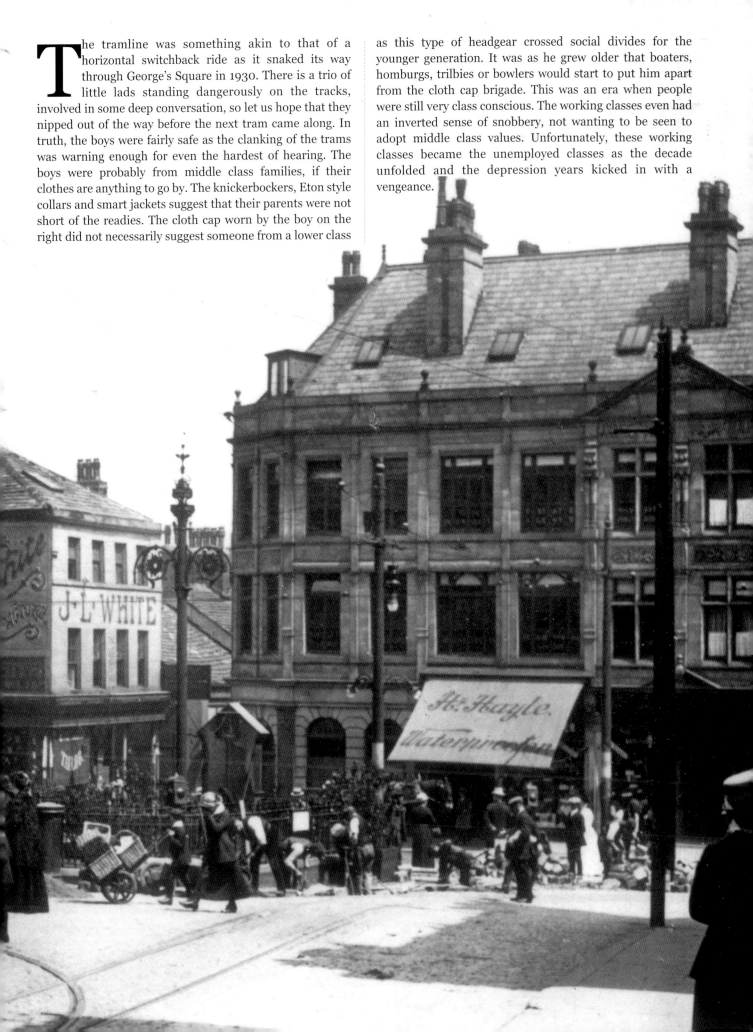

Below: Luddenden Foot is situated on Burnley Road, halfway between Sowerby Bridge and Mytholmroyd. The large mill that can be seen belonged to British Furtex. The company manufactured moquette upholstery fabrics whose primary use was for seat coverings within the transport industry. It changed hands a number of times, having been owned by the Homfray Carpets Group under Denis Gillam until the 1970s and then sold to John Lawrence before being acquired by Melton Medes in June, 1987. The shops are all delightful period pieces, with some intriguing notices that tell us something about life and times in the 20s. One outlet operated as the Halifax Corporation Tram Parcel Office, reminding us that those public transport vehicles sometimes carried more than just passengers. There was a public telephone available for use. Few homes had their own phones and the idea of one that could slip into your pocket was just too fanciful to contemplate. One sign advertises 'Sewing machine orders taken here'. Women used treadle machines to make their own clothes and curtains, saving money that the middle classes would spend on such items in Halifax's department stores. As a newspaper billboard states 'How to view the eclipse', we know that the photograph was taken just before 29 June 1927, as on that day a narrow, marginal eclipse lasting about 30 seconds was visible across Britain and Scandinavia over a path just 50 miles in width.

Above: This 1930s view looking north long Market Street from Union Street is still instantly recognisable, despite the many changes down the decades since the photograph was taken. Along the left of the picture is the bottom side of Halifax's market hall, the finest remaining example of its kind in Britain. In the centre of the scene is the top of Woolshops and the town's oldest remaining shop. Commonly referred to as the 'Tudor' building, suggesting a date in the 16th century, it actually carries a datestone for 1670. Both are probably wrong; the official listing suggests it is 'probably early 17th century'. Almost all of the other buildings along the right hand of the picture were replaced during improvements in the 1970s and 1980s. The schoolboy walking along the pavement on the right is a reminder of the important distinction between boys and men in those days: short trousers versus long. Until the 1960s boys were generally expected to wear short trousers well into their teenage years. Being taken to buy one's first pair of long trousers was an important rite of passage. The first boy into long trousers gained enormous prestige – the last, a sense of shame deep enough to last a lifetime.

Above: On 28 February, 1931. This chilly scene in Todmorden was captured by Thomas Greenlees, the Church Street saddler. The Town Hall is just visible on the right, and in the background can be seen the old White Hart. Though by the 1930s motor vehicles were predominant on the roads horse-drawn wagons such as this were still commonplace. In fact they were about to get even more common rather than less, as the great Depression began to bite and the increasing affluence of the Roaring Twenties gave way to a decade of mass unemployment and increasing poverty. Despite the invention of the internal combustion engine in the latter part of the 19th century there will still many decades to go before horses would cease to be a familiar sight on our roads –for some reason rag and bone men were the final trade to dispense with one of man's oldest friends.

Top right, facing page: Thornton Square Brighouse pictured in the 1930s. To the right, with its prominent clock, is Brighouse Town Hall built in 1887. Though easy to imagine that Thornton Square has always existed it was still relatively new when this scene was captured for posterity. Until 1912 what became Thornton Square had been largely occupied by Holroyd Buildings which were demolished to allow traffic to move more smoothly through the town centre to and from Rastrick. The Square was named after the Mayor, Alderman Robert Thornton, who paid for the

On 21 January, 2008 Brighouse was hit by floods. One of the worst hit areas was in the town centre where the fast-rising River Calder burst its banks in a number of places. The area around Briggate and Mill Royd Street was under two feet of water and many motorists were forced to abandon their vehicles. It wasn't the first time Brighouse had been flooded. A far worse flood had hit the town in the 19th century, the high-water mark being commemorated by being etched on a wall at the canal basin.

clock above the town hall. Until the creation of Brighouse's first bus station on this site, buses would simply park in the centre of the open space. Two buses are featured here, one an old single-decker from the early 1920s, whilst in the foreground a 'modern' double-decker. Bus design was still in its development stage, although designers had got around to enclosing the upper deck they had clearly not yet thought that it might also be a good idea to enclose the stairs leading to it. In the 1930s travelling by bus was still a daily experience for the vast majority of people. In the morning rush and in the evenings it was standing room only, and woe betide the poor soul who had slept in. There were surely few more miserable experiences than getting

to the bus only to be told by the conductor 'sorry full up'. By the 1930s buses posed a serious threat to trams which had ruled the roost for three decades. Many rural routes opened in this decade which revitalised many of Calderdale's outlying villages.

This photograph, believed to be of the floods of 1947, was taken in Thornton Square looking across to Briggate and over Anchor Bridge to Rastrick. The cameraman seems to have been standing outside the Black Bull Hotel, one of the oldest pubs in Brighouse. To the left, immediately before the bridge, is the aptly named Ship Street, which now forms the market place – the buildings no longer exist though those in the left foreground are largely unaltered. The nearest building on the right was demolished and new buildings erected on the site in the 1970s whilst across the river the nearest buildings are the Anchor Inn and Assembly Rooms. Beyond, all buildings have long since been demolished to provide car parking. Drivers attempting to take this same route into Thornton Square today will be foiled: floods or no floods. In the 1980s the entrance from Briggate was blocked off, diverting all traffic around the town centre along Owler Ings Road.

Warley is as delightful a village as it was in the interwar years when children hopped aboard the single decker bus that bounced along the cobbles as it took them to school. Its history goes back so far that it was included in the Domesday Book, where it was referred to as 'Werlafeslei'. Warley Town, as this particular area is known, was originally one of 23 townships in the old Halifax parish. It was also one of the largest, stretching down to Luddenden and over to Sowerby Bridge. It was made up of tiny hamlets and little farming communities. A third of its population was wiped out by the Great Plague in the 14th century and it suffered some damage from skirmishes during the English Civil War. Local names such as Camp End and Sentry Edge provide a link with more difficult times.

resident. Wilfred Pickles (pictured bottom left) who lived here for some years. Wilfred was the star of the long running radio show 'Have A Go', with its famous catchphrase 'Give him the money, Mabel' when someone won a prize in the quiz.

Left: This charming scene depicts four twelve-year-old boys next to the Maypole in Warley. They are reading an article about Wilfred Pickles about to transmit the 'Have A Go' programme from his native village. Edward Riley, the boy second from the left, was showing a particular interest in the Evening Courier. This proved prophetic as he later became the paper's editor!

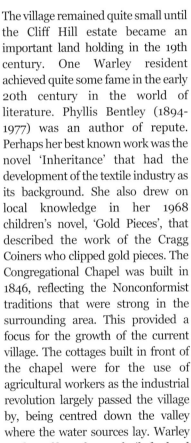

The village remained quite small until the Cliff Hill estate became an important land holding in the 19th century. One Warley resident achieved quite some fame in the early 20th century in the world of literature. Phyllis Bentley (1894-1977) was an author of repute. Perhaps her best known work was the novel 'Inheritance' that had the development of the textile industry as its background. She also drew on local knowledge in her 1968 children's novel, 'Gold Pieces', that described the work of the Cragg Coiners who clipped gold pieces. The Congregational Chapel was built in 1846, reflecting the Nonconformist traditions that were strong in the surrounding area. This provided a focus for the growth of the current village. The cottages built in front of the chapel were for the use of agricultural workers as the industrial revolution largely passed the village by, being centred down the valley where the water sources lay. Warley also became a site for a number of large houses built for local businessmen who wanted to live close to their enterprises, but far enough away to escape the smoke and grime of Halifax itself. The present Maypole Inn is a reminder of the great maypole, the last one ever seen in Calderdale, that was erected in front of the chapel in 1863. It replaced an earlier one that had been erected around 1814 to celebrate the defeat of Napoleon. Unfortunately, the one in the photograph only lasted about 25 years and was removed as it had deteriorated rather badly. Older readers might remember another former Warley

Right: There may well be a string of antique shops and cafes, but there is a lot more to Hebden Bridge. During the industrial revolution the water from the hills helped turn the mill wheels and promoted prosperity in the area. The steep sided valleys gave rise to the interesting architectural development of 'double decker' housing as textile workers battled with the terrain to build their homes. It became so well known for its clothing trade, that some nicknamed it 'trouser town'! Yet, Hebden Bridge was still within a few minutes of rolling countryside and the stunning views across the moorlands beyond, and it is the same today. There is a lovely mix of the rural and the gently urban. The old packhorse bridge was instrumental in the naming of the village that grew around this crossing point over Hebden Water. It was here that packhorse routes from Rochdale, Burnley and Heptonstall to Halifax converged.

Below: For decade upon decade Greenwood's bookshop at Bull Green was a Halifax institution. With the bus stop from all points west dropping off passengers almost outside its door the shop was a magnet for thousands of customers each week. Though this picture is undated it is clearly a reminder of Greenwood's in the earlier years of the 20th century. Among the unusual features seen here are the twin gas lights in front of the shop: gas pipes emerge from above the shop window, whilst the lights themselves feature large on-off switches which could be operated using a long pole. It seems unlikely that such large, vulnerable, glass globes would survive long in today's rowdier times, any more than would the display model outdoor thermometer. Modern readers may be mystified by the 'Library' sign hanging above the thermometer. Libraries today are virtually the exclusive province of local authorities and other public institutions. In the past however private subscription libraries were commonplace, and many, if not most, booksellers ran their own private libraries. In later decades the shopfront and interior would be wholly modernised. For children no start at secondary school was complete without a visit to Greenwood's to acquire essential supplies and equipment.

Right: Nearly half a century ago, the policeman on point duty was a regular sight on Commercial Street and many other busy parts of town. Traffic congestion was becoming an ever increasing problem as private car ownership boomed in the Harold Macmillan 'never had it so good' years. There must have been something very satisfying about being able to demonstrate a power that could bring traffic to a standstill as he imperiously motioned pedestrians across the road. With just one sweep of a white sleeved arm he signalled traffic forward along the street or permitted it to join from the side. Whenever he pointed at you, it was if he was mimicking the famous World War One poster of Lord Kitchener, 'Your country needs you.' He did not need whistles and wild gestures like his continental counterparts. He was calm and, of course, British. At first, point duty was a fairly comfortable if boring job, with little traffic on the streets. However, it became almost a mathematical exercise as the proliferation of motor cars presented the policeman with the need for eyes in the back of his head. He must also have suffered from breathing in the fumes from the exhausts of cars that emitted much more poisonous gases than they are allowed to now.

Here's a photo of Bull Green, looking across to Cow Green, taken in the 1960s. Many changes have taken place: not least in the volume of traffic. The road along Cow Green has become a dual carriageway, and the planted area immediately in front of the camera has become a car park. In the far distance can be seen the spire of All Souls' church at Woodside. Amongst the businesses opposite are a radio and electrical engineers, an antiques shop and Sutcliffe's Coal Office. The nearest building is the Crown and Anchor pub, with the side entrance to its once-popular Adega Bar just out of sight.

The school was built in 1863 from money donated by Sir Francis Crossley and Mr Porter. In recent years the pupils took it upon themselves to sell sponsored 'minutes' and thus raised enough money to pay for the restoration of the clock.King Cross Methodist Church, in front of the school, is still there but all the buildings between the church and the bottom of Warley Road have now been demolished in order to create a traffic light complex. Streets of terraced houses edging King Cross and the bottom of Warley Road have also been taken down and this has made space for grassy areas. The Alan Fold public house can be seen at the right hand edge of this photograph and there used to be a police station in this vicinity. The Halifax Fire Station is now located opposite King Cross Methodist Church on the road leading up towards Savile Park. The Fire Station used to be located on Gibbet Street and one local alderman was once honoured by having a fire engine named after him. At the naming ceremony, Alderman Fred Sharp recalled an incident when he had once almost been run down by a fire engine during his term office as Mayor of Halifax.

Below: Even at the start of the 1960s, some attempts were made to regulate the flow of traffic in and around the town centre. Waterhouse Street became one way and the police were involved on point duty as part of the plans to keep things moving. More dramatic moves, such as the building of Burdock Way a decade later and the eventual pedestrianisation of portions of the shopping areas, were yet to be considered. The building on the left, by the zebra crossing, was part of the National Provincial Bank, founded in late 1833 in Gloucester. Within three years it was given permission to print its own banknotes. By 1900, there were 250 branches and this expansion continued until in 1918 when it joined with the Union of London and Smiths Bank. In 1970 it merged with Westminster Bank to create National Westminster Bank, or NatWest as it is now known. Waterhouse Street took its name from the family who owned Shibden Hall in the 16th century.

Left: Commercial Street, as the name suggests, has a number of fairly important buildings along its length that have had quite a bit to do with the town's economy. In the distance are the old District Bank Chambers that now house Bramley's estate agency. The current Lloyds TSB building is in the centre. Opposite this bank, on the near side of Rawson Street, is the store that has Yorkshire written through and through it. Harvey's is one of those family run department stores that has disappeared from so many towns across our country and been replaced by the giant chains and the supermarket clothing departments. Our favourite town centre store was founded in the 1920s by E T Harvey in a small unit in Dewsbury. By the 1950s it had expanded to another three shops in Halifax, Wakefield and Harrogate. The Rawson Street store was opened in 1950 on the site of the old Waddington's Dress Warehouse and ran as a ladies' fashion shop selling clothing and accessories. Harvey's is a true family business in that the current managing director, Tracy Harvey, is a direct descendant of the founder. Tracy's partners on the board include her parents Roger and Sue and her brother Richard.

Above: A view over the King Cross area taken from Warley Road, a dramatically changed part of Halifax. The clock tower of the Crossley Heath School, formerly Crossley and Porter Grammar School, can be seen poking up against the skyline.

Above: The Feathers Hotel on Haugh Shaw Road, King Cross seen in 1968, was part of the Webster's Brewery empire. A pint of 'Webby's' was one of the premier tastes in beer drinking in those days. Even over the border in Lancashire, drinkers with discerning taste buds enjoyed quaffing ales that were among the finest that Yorkshire could brew. Samuel Webster opened his Fountain Head Brewery at Ovenden in 1838. Situated near a natural spring, this water source provided for the brewery needs for many years. Websters merged with Joseph Stocks in 1932 and continued to operate as a very profitable company well on after the last war. Its premier brands, Yorkshire Bitter and Green Label, a light mild, were feted across the north. The brewery had a large number of tied houses, including the Feathers. It expanded its business in the 1950s when entering into a contract to manufacture Guinness. A further merger was negotiated with J Hey of Bradford in 1966, but by the end of the decade, the big boys were in town. This was a period that saw many breweries, even very successful ones, come to the attention of the large behemoths of the trade. Takeovers became commonplace and Webster's became part of Watney Mann in 1971 and, later still, Scottish Newcastle. The brewery closed in 1996 with the loss of many jobs. Some readers might recall the amusing television adverts that had two talking dray horses, Uncle and Nephew, extolling the virtues of Webster's beer.

Right: Here's a long ago scene of commercial barge traffic on the River Calder at Brighouse. A barge is just about to enter the lock leading from the river into the Brighouse canal basin. Straddling the river is 'Ha'penny Bridge' one of many similarly named bridges in the British Isles. The name comes from the half-penny toll once charged to cross. In the background the two mills have had different fates: the building on the right has been demolished to make way for a supermarket; the central building has been converted into modern luxury flats with an additional penthouse storey added. The Calder and Hebble Navigation, runs for more than 20 mils miles from the Aire and Calder Navigation at Wakefield to Sowerby Bridge. Around half of the 'navigation' was on the River Calder, with locks to by-pass weirs. There were eventually two lengthy canals, from Calder Grove to Ravensthorpe and between Brighouse and Sowerby Bridge. Work to make the River Calder

navigable above Wakefield began in 1758. The navigation reached Sowerby Bridge by 1770. The trans-pennine Rochdale Canal section to Manchester from Sowerby Bridge was completed in 1804. A branch to Halifax from Salterhebble, closely following the course of the River Hebble, was opened in 1828, rising 110 feet to a terminus behind Halifax Railway Station. Most of the Halifax branch, on which there were no fewer than 14, was closed in 1942. Most commercial traffic had ended by the mid-1950s. Today pleasure boats have replaced commerce.

Below: Pye Nest contains housing estates that are sandwiched between Rochdale Road and Wakefield Road, just above the centre of Sowerby Bridge. Many of the street names around this district bear testament to the former environment of the locality. Pye Nest refers to magpies, but some other names are much clearer in their meaning. Crow Wood Park, Willow Gardens and Woodland Drive require no explanation. This 1962 photograph was taken at a time when life in Britain was changing irrevocably. The establishment was under threat as society demanded a new focus. We had come through the austerity of the 1950s and now it was time to look forward to a brighter future. The unique sight of Wainhouse Tower jutting up into the sky continued to be a major scenic feature, just as it had since 1875.

Above right: The Tower pictured was illuminated to show off all its glory during the celebrations for the Queen's silver jubilee in 1977. As the street parties were taking place, the lights from the famous folly could be seen from many miles away. The imposing structure was commissioned by Edward Wainhouse (1817-1883). He owned the Washer Lane Dye Works and a Parliamentary Act of 1870 was passed as one of the measures

intended to curb pollution in our towns and cities. Living conditions in Victorian England, with its grime, soot and smoke, were very poor, especially for the working classes. Owners were now required to build tall chimneys so that the smoke from their factories could be carried away from the built-up areas and out of the valleys. This chimney was built in the period 1871-75, but Wainhouse sold his business to his works manager in 1874. The latter refused to pay the building costs, so Wainhouse kept it for himself to use as an observatory. The elaborate galleries at the top of the tower and the upper section were completed by architect Richard Swarbrick Dugdale, who replaced the original designer, Isaac Booth, when Wainhouse severed links with the dye works. The final building costs are estimated to be in the region of £15,000. After Wainhouse's death, the tower was sold by auction. However, a public subscription was raised after World War I and the folly thus came into the Corporation's ownership in 1919. The slim tower rises 275 feet into the sky and, on occasions, is open to the general public.

Above and below: In 2001 this scene changed significantly with the appearance of the Barum Top Inn, a pub in the JD Wetherspoon chain. For many decades, however, the site was connected with the motor trade, before a relatively brief life as a carpet showroom. In both these photographs the cameraman is standing at Bull Green looking at the same building from a slightly different angle. The older of the two pictures is from the 1950s, at which time the building at the corner of Rawson Street and Barum Top was occupied by the Olympia Garage. The roadbed is still cobbled and double yellow line and 'no parking' zones were far in the future. Cars came in any colour you liked – so long as they were black. 'Street furniture' looks decidedly sparse compared to the clutter of today. The belisha beacon which marks the pedestrian crossing was named after Leslie Hore-Belisha (1895-1957), the Minister of Transport who introduced the first of them in 1934. Zebra crossings were first used (after some isolated experiments) at 1,000 sites in Britain in 1949 (the original pattern being alternating strips of blue and yellow), and in 1951 they were introduced into law, though would take some years more to appear in Halifax town centre. By the 1970s the former Olympia Garage had evolved into the Austin House car showroom of Thomas Greenwood's Sons Ltd. Pride of place in the photo goes to the phenomenally successful 'Mini', whilst the other gleaming models on display will inevitably bring back memories among readers who once drove similar vehicles.

Below: In the swinging 60s we saw something of a revolution, particularly among the younger generation. As a group of people with money in their pockets, they became an economic force with which to be reckoned. They also eschewed many of the norms of society to which their parents clung. No longer would young people be happy to dress in the same way that they mums and dads had done. They demanded their own fashions and set their own standards in terms of morality as well. Young people did not view getting married and raising the conventional 2.4 children as the be all and end all of life.

She loves you yeah, yeah, yeah was all well and good, but the wedding ring and the pram, seen here on the left of the bench, was something that could wait or might never be needed at all. The middle aged group sitting and gazing across Bull Green did not know what the world was coming to. These people had been born in an era when you did as authority told you, without question. Now those values were under threat. As the decade rolled on they would call for the reintroduction of National Service. At least that would mean that some of those long haired lads would get a decent short back and sides!

Above: Crossing the road at Wards End in the 1950s, these cinemagoers would be amazed to know that Halifax would be unable to boast a picture house of its own in the first years of the next century. When these family groups were looking for entertainment, a session at the 'flicks' was always close to the top of the list. They had just left the Gaumont on Wards End, one of several excellent picture houses that Halifax once had. The Regal was across the road and the Odeon was on Broad Street, on the other side of town. The Gaumont took its name in 1948, having been originally known as The Picture House. Under this title, it showed its first silent films and shorts in 1913. It was one of the first-purpose built cinemas. Previously, films had been shown in church halls, schoolrooms and converted theatres. With the advent of sound in 1929, cinema going entered its golden period with packed houses every night as customers flocked to see the latest Hollywood heartthrobs appear on screen. The Gaumont was renamed the Astra in 1973, but that did not help rally falling audiences. It closed in 1982 and was replaced by the Coliseum nightclub.

Bottom left, facing page: King Cross in the swinging 60s was full of little, individual retail outlets, just like any other district of Halifax. Perhaps surprisingly, although the businesses in the photograph are no longer with us, the old part of King Cross Road still has such stores that mark it out as something of a shopping oasis. This is even more remarkable when considering the proximity of the large Tesco supermarket on the other side of Aachen Way. Such large stores were still for the future when this scene was captured. Shoppers went from one outlet to another to do their weekly restocking of the larder. Some housewives would be going off along the street, with their wicker baskets cradled in the crook of their arms, on a more regular basis to buy fresh vegetables and bread. Butchers, greengrocers and confectioners traded side by side and each shopkeeper knew his regulars by name. The days of self service were yet to come and it was the personal touch that we all enjoyed.

Above and below: This pair of photographs shows a before and after scenario. They are quite patently taken from the same spot, but many years apart. Looking along Stainland Road from Little Bradley and into West Vale, the old West Vale Station can be seen on the right in the older picture. The line belonged to the Lancashire and Yorkshire Railway Company, so named in 1847 after the Manchester and Leeds Railway absorbed a number of smaller and earlier local companies. It served the industrial heartland of the northwest of England, providing important connections across the Pennines for the Victorian entrepreneurs and businessmen of the day. As its influence expanded, the railway company developed an extensive and complex system and developed its own interests in shipping off both the northwest coast and in the North Sea. A huge freight business was built up to accompany the large commuter network and massive influx of holidaymakers on their way to Blackpool and around Morecambe Bay. The trans-Pennine express that linked Liverpool with York, via Manchester, Bradford and Leeds, was an outstanding example of Victorian enterprise. The Lancashire and Yorkshire Railway became part of the London, Midland and Scottish Railway at the beginning of 1923 when 'the big four' companies were formed. Speak's large mill, on the left, burned down in 1980, not long before the more modern photograph was snapped on 9 April that year. In the newer scene, the railway station yard has been replaced by a housing estate. The woodland above these homes is on Hullen Edge and, behind the trees, the nine hole Elland Golf Club sits perched on a small plateau, looking down and across Stainland Road to one of its rival courses, Bradley Hall. The Elland Club has Nick Kryzwicki as its professional. His father, Ryszard Lech Kryzwicki, was a well known soccer player who appeared on the international scene when representing his country. Those who are not aficionados of the beautiful game would guess forever at his nationality without ever arriving at the answer. Known to most as Dick, young Ryszard was born in Flintshire in 1947 and won eight caps for Wales in a career that saw him play for West Bromwich Albion, Huddersfield Town, Scunthorpe, Northampton and Lincoln.

Marshalls - A Name Set in Stone

You won't see many stone roses at the Royal Horticultural Society's Chelsea Flower Show. But visitors will see plenty of other stone products from the Show's main sponsor: Marshalls plc, a local firm with an international reputation.

Established in the late 1880s, Marshalls, one of the Halifax area's best known business names, is now Britain's leading manufacturer of superior natural stone and innovative concrete hard landscaping products, supplying the construction, home improvement and landscape markets. The company provides the product ranges, design services, technical expertise, ideas and inspiration to transform gardens, drives and public and commercial landscapes.

The Marshalls Group operates its own quarries and manufacturing sites, as well as 12 service centres and 14 offices throughout the UK. As a major plc, Marshalls is committed to quality in everything it does, including environmental best practice and continual improvement in health and safety performance for the benefit of its 3,000-strong workforce.

Solomon Marshall (1847-1914) lived at Hove Edge, Brighouse, with his wife Sarah, whom he had married in 1870. They had nine children. Solomon was a foreman at Pond Quarry, in Brighouse, where he learned his trade. He served as a Brighouse Councillor, an indication of his high standing in the community. By 1895 Solomon had seen that a good living could be made from quarrying and decided to set up on his own.

In the prospering late-Victorian era there was plenty of demand for building materials and Solomon worked land at Southgates quarrying for stone.

There are two types of useful stone in the Halifax district, found under an 'overburden' of 50 feet, both of which have been extensively quarried. Ashlar stone has little 'lamination' and is suitable for carving and moulding into windowsills, coping stones, mullions and transoms. Beyond, and beneath another 10 foot layer of shale, can be found Hard York Stone or 'Elland Edge Flagstone' which is, by contrast, well laminated and can easily be split along its lamination planes to provide a smooth finish over quite large areas, and so was particularly suited for paving flags, steps and kerbstones.

Mining to a depth of 60 feet or more, and working across an eight-foot bed of Ashlar, the business served Solomon well.

On 21 March, 1904, the firm was formally registered by Solomon and his five sons, Hanson, Ernest, John, Wilson and Norman, as S. Marshall & Sons Ltd in accordance with the Companies Acts of 1862 and 1900.

Top left: Solomon Marshall. Below left: Early top dressers. Above: S. Marshall & Sons Articles of Association. Below: Douglas Marshall with the largest landing produced, 1936.

reputation was such that export orders were received from as far afield as Hamburg.

Solomon Marshall died ten years after the firm he founded had been incorporated. Later his grandchildren came to work with their fathers in the family business.

Harold, Douglas, Geoffrey, Harry and Herbert all joined the firm from the age of 15. The company now had a rich blend of new skills which would play an important part in the growth of the business. Harold would eventually become Chairman, Douglas the Managing Director of the Concrete

In those early days Hanson Marshall, who had followed in his father's footsteps as Councillor and Mayor of Brighouse, began buying land to sustain stone reserves for the company. The first land acquired in Southowram was bought in 1910 at the site of the current manufacturing facility at West Lane. Here the stone was quarried, then skilfully dressed into kerbs, walling, setts and paving.

Father and sons worked together to quarry stone, and they prospered, selling to borough councils as far away as London, transporting the materials by canal and railway. The firm's

*Top: Brookfoot works in 1939. **Above left:** Douglas and his father Hanson looking at their first air drill, 1936. **Left:** The company's first flag press, 1937.*

and Quarries Division, Geoffrey the Managing Director of the Engineering Division, Harry would become Company Secretary and Herbert the Quarrying Director.

Strong competition meant that the firm constantly sought to increase its efficiency. A major advance at the time was a move away from steam powered cranes to electric cranes in 1922 – Marshalls would be the first company in Yorkshire to make that transition. All the cranes were manufactured locally by William Bradley of Rastrick.

The continuing success of the company led to expansion, which included the acquisition of Brier Lodge from Hanson Freeman, a local landowner. The site would become the headquarters of the Landscape Division until 2003, and a key manufacturing site which remains to this day.

By the 1930s the company was working the land at its Brookfoot and Cromwell sites, areas which were now being developed extensively by electric crane and gangs of skilled masons. As the resources of the area were finite however, the company began to

look at ways of capitalising on its competitive advantages, which included its efficiency.

The company had introduced the use of compressed air to power its drills, a significant step forward in a very labour-intensive industry. Again Marshalls was the firm in the area to make this step forward. At the time the process of 'winning the stone' as it was known produced some waste, not only limiting the way in which stone could be quarried, as some stone had to be left to support the 'roof', but also because so much stone could not be used once the masons had split the product into materials suitable for building. S Marshall & Sons recognised this problem and began to sell the unused stone at a reduced price to Brookes, a competitor based in nearby Hipperholme, the firm used the

Top: West Lane pictured in 1954. **Above left:** Machine moulding of concrete flagstones in the early 1960s. **Below:** A bird's eye view of Marshalls' Southowram quarry in 1962. **Below inset:** The company's first Halco-Stenuick drill.

unused stone in its concrete paving plant. Recycling became an important consideration, and remains so to this day.

When the agreement with Brookes came to an end Harold and Douglas Marshall decided to buy a flag press, and began to crush the unused stone, mixing it with cement and water to create pressed flags. This was Marshalls' first venture into manufacturing concrete paving. Despite derision from other quarrying firms this ingenious method of using unused aggregate material gave the company a new competitive edge, and the concrete business grew. S Marshall & Sons Ltd patented its new product 'Marshalite Artificial Stone' on 1 June, 1937, and production began at the Brookfoot site later that year.

The company pressed moulded flags at a pressure of 1,555 lbs per square inch. Laboratory test results impressed road engineers when they confirmed the strength and performance of the innovative new product.

Like so many businesses the outbreak of war in 1939 saw the company's entirely male workforce depleted by service in the armed forces. Both the firm and the building industry suffered from the labour shortage.

S Marshall & Sons production fell dramatically, and its workforce was reduced to just 24. The company survived under these conditions until the end on the war in 1945, when, due to huge demand for building materials, the company had a fine opportunity to rebuild both itself and the country.

In 1947 a second production site opened at West Lane producing lintels, steps and fence posts. The business grew rapidly through the development of methods of mass manufacture and a growing demand for concrete products as an alternative to natural stone. Capable of pressing and pre-casting concrete, the possibilities for broadening its product range gave the company a significant edge over its competitors and offered many new opportunities.

Another significant innovation in the post-war years would assure the company a place as an industry leader.

During his service in the Second World War Herbert Marshall had made the acquaintance of a Belgian engineer. The Belgian had told him about 'down the hole' drilling equipment,

*Top left: Hand-splitting of slabs to form kerbs, 1962. **Top right:** Finishing the surface of a stone with a broad chisel, 1962. **Below:** Ken Crabtree takes delivery of one of the new Marshalls trucks of the 1960s.*

something which would radically improve Marshalls' operation. An agreement was signed with Stenuick Frere to manufacture 'Quarry and Waterwell' drilling machines, the beginning of Halco-Stenuick Drills. These new drills were capable of drilling to a depth of 70 feet, far beyond anything that had previously been possible. The advancement in drilling methods was not the only advantage the business now enjoyed. The ability to manufacture tungsten carbide drill bits, which were in high demand at a time of shortages and rationing, enhanced the company's efficiency significantly. This resource led to the establishment of an engineering division in 1948. The innovations and developments from this company division would be fundamental to Marshalls further development.

The demand for an increasingly varied product line was met by the company developing products using mixed aggregates, colours and cement – the process giving S Marshal & Sons a major advantage over many of its rivals. Those successful product ranges were largely due to the foresight of product development teams and a skilled workforce, as much as to opportunity. The success of Marshalite Walling, for example, owed its inspiration to a broken flag.

In 1952 the aesthetic of a broken flag which resembled a natural stone face and texture inspired the development of a new walling product, the demand for which would grow to over 20 million blocks per year. The ability to replicate natural stone products and produce them to an exceptionally high standard is at the heart of the company's success. In 1955, imitating the riven face of natural stone resulted in the development of another hugely

successful product, Pennine Paving. This was the first wet cast concrete product which would dominate the garden market for years. Both Pennine Paving and Marshalite Walling stimulated an interest in the growth of domestic garden design, a new market then, but one which has seen staggering growth to reach its position today.

A further example of the firm's pioneering approach was the introduction of Screen Walling in the 1960s, which introduced an original, imaginative and decorative product to the market.

Such was the confidence in Marshalls' manufacturing methods that additional investment was sought to enable the company to take its next vital step forward. There was a thriving market for building materials, but transport costs were high. S Marshall & Sons planned to expand its manufacturing base nationally by making acquisitions closer to the source of the aggregates it used, and nearer to densely populated areas. The decision was made to float the company on the stock exchange in 1964 with a share price of 12 shillings and sixpence. S Marshall & Sons then became Marshalls Halifax plc.

The company acquired Stockton Stone & Concrete, Norton and Wm Heaton & Co, Maltby in 1969, followed a year later by Brookes, based just across the valley from Marshalls original site at West Lane. The latter acquisition was a reflection of just how far Marshalls had progressed, as Brookes had been a key competitor since 1904 with a major share of the market.

In 1972, due to a downturn in the home building market, Marshalls' concrete brick presses were stopped. It was decided to

Top: A newspaper feature of vehicular paving on offer from Marshalls: standard hydraulically pressed pimple finish and in the attractive machine rubbed surface of Perfecta Paving. *Above:* Marshalls working with Ling Bob School children on the creation of their Sensory Garden. *Left:* Groups of school children regularly visit Marshalls and are given a guided tour of the site and a general overview of activities.

experiment producing block paving at the recently acquired Maltby site, which led to another product diversification for the company. Adding to its portfolio of firsts the company developed the 'Beany Block' which combined drain and kerb in a single unit. Marshalls was also the first to automate edge stacking of paving, and the first to use recycled water in the production process.

The 1980s saw property prices soar, and also growth in the DIY market which in turn allowed for tremendous growth within the company. It was a boom time for many industries, and one which saw Marshalls' most rapid rate of growth, allowing the firm to achieve its goal of becoming a nationwide business.

Strategic acquisitions saw the company now expand to include a network of manufacturing sites encompassing clay, natural stone, flag and kerb, block paving and many more commercial and domestic products. Expansion even saw the company buying factories in the USA, an American subsidiary which Marshalls' would operate for a decade.

But beyond mere business Marshalls and its workforce maintain a keen commitment to giving back to the

community. Over the last 10 years, for example, Marshalls employees have donated no less than £250,000 to charities of their own choice. At Ling Bob School, Halifax, Marshalls offered materials and labour to help create a themed landscape garden complete with stage, seating and vegetable patch. At Elland Park canal lock Marshsalls staff planted dozens of shrubs and hundreds of bulbs on both sides of the canal. The company also helped restore the main emblem for Todmorden Railway Station which had become badly dilapidated down the years.

Nor are these the only community initiatives contributed to by Marshalls, similar commitment is replicated far and wide, wherever the firm has a presence.

Marshalls had grown far beyond anything Solomon Marshall could ever have imagined, with five generations of his family

each having played their part in ensuring the firm's success whilst still retaining the family values of which it is so proud. A testament to those values is the long list of fathers, sons, brothers and sisters who have shared Marshalls as a workplace and the long list of employees who have competed 25-years service or more.

Today Marshalls plc is the UK's leading manufacturer of superior, innovative, natural stone and concrete products, supplying the construction, home improvement and landscape markets. The company provides the product ranges, design services, technical expertise, ideas and inspiration to transform and redefine landscapes and the built environment.

The company's core values underpin the business. Every individual is equally important, and Marshalls values the contribution that every one of its dedicated and skilled workforce makes. Innovation, critical to the firm's strategy, allows Marshalls to deliver the highest quality products, as it has been doing for over a hundred years.

Left: Neil Davidson accepting the 2007 award from the National Payroll Giving Awards for the contributions from Marshalls staff to their chosen charities. **Top:** A natural stone donation from Marshalls to the world famous Brighouse and Rastrick Brass Band. **Below:** Marshalls sponsored the Maxi 50 Mile Challenge in May 2007. Marshalls Brookfoot entered two teams in the South Pennine Challenge. Pictured are some of the walkers with the Chief Executive.

THE WAR YEARS

Good old Winnie! That was what our parents and grandparents shouted during the last war. He was not just the country's figurehead, he was its real leader for the vast majority of those six long years of strife. He was a popular replacement for the naïve Neville Chamberlain whose indecision had helped precipitate the war. Winston Churchill was seen as the saviour and when he entered 10 Downing Street our forebears knew that this was the right move. Even during the darkest hours, the evacuation at Dunkirk, the Blitz, the loss of Singapore and all the other trials and tribulations that had to be endured, with Churchill at the helm it seemed that it would all turn out tickety-boo. His eternal optimism, stirring speeches and V sign helped public morale no end. When the war was over a General Election was held as there had been a coalition government previously. 'Help him finish the job', was the slogan reminding the electorate that Churchill was the man who helped win the war and now he could win the peace. He came to Lister Lane as part of his promotional tour and addressed the crowd with his usual uplifting oratory and continued across the country in the same vein. Yet, there is nothing more fickle than the British public. It said, 'Thanks, but no thanks' and the Labour Party, under Clement Attlee, swept to power in a victory that rocked Churchill to the very butt of his cigar.

Right: Watch out, Dr Who, the Cybermen are on the way. Well, perhaps this photograph was an inspiration for the scriptwriters of the popular television show, but in 1941 these soldiers were for real, not make believe. The experience of men in the trenches in the Great War led many to believe that chemical warfare was a real threat. This time, with lessons learned from the Spanish Civil War, the country knew that aerial bombardment would be something with which we would have to reckon. That those bombs might contain poisonous gases was something we could not ignore, so civil defence groups quickly organised practices and drills in the event of an onslaught by the enemy. Gas masks were issued to civilians and service personnel alike, with particular emphasis to those living in heavily populated and industrial areas, the probable focus of attack. All schoolchildren were issued with them in the early summer of 1939 and they carried them in purpose built boxes to and from lessons. Babies also had special helmets into which mothers would have to pump air with a bellows.

Below: A grand spectacle for the people of Halifax on this occasion - the celebrations of the 250th anniversary of Halifax's own Duke of Wellington's Regiment. For the first time since Waterloo Day, (June 18), 1945 the Dukes exercised their right to march through the town with bayonets fixed, Colours flying and bands playing. The date is the 24th May, 1952. This photograph shows Lt-Colonel JF Crossley, MBE, TD, in his comet tank leading the 382nd Field Regiment, RA, Duke of Wellington's. The 24th May that year dawned hot and sunny and the people of the town turned out in their thousands to celebrate with the Dukes. The parade began at 2 pm, the crowds, an hour earlier, were already estimated at 20,000. This shot was taken at the top of Crown Street. Can any readers spot themselves in the crowd? The highway is paved with 'sets' and the zebra crossing in the bottom right hand corner would have had a belisha beacon at each end. The Dukes regimental museum is housed at Bankfield Museum in Akroyd Park and has exhibits covering all the major exploits of the 'Havercake Lads.' The regiment will celebrate its 300th anniversary in 2002 and, although the style of the celebration has not yet been decided, the people of the town will no doubt play a part.

Left: Shibden Hall Home Guard was one of many such brigades who promised to stand between us and the might of the Nazi empire should the anticipated invasion of Britain take place in the early 1940s. The popular BBC TV sitcom 'Dad's Army' made audiences laugh in the 1970s and 1980s. The country's living rooms rocked to viewers' merriment at the antics of a Home Guard unit run by a pompous bank manager, but the television series was unfair to these men. The Home Guard was not the bumbling outfit as portrayed by the fictitious Warmington on Sea platoon. Admittedly, when initially formed as the Local Defence Volunteers, some early efforts were ridiculous. One platoon patrolled with imitation rifles once used in a Drury Lane production. Elsewhere catapults were recommended as launching pads for petrol bombs and broomsticks were converted into pikes when knives were attached. The force was renamed the Home Guard in July 1940 and 250,000 men were enrolled. Although still handicapped by a shortage of weapons and resources, they trained with vigour and initiative. Here, Shibden men held their rifles and bayonets with pride and this group even had a machine gun in its armoury. Their resolve was just as firm as any enlisted man and that determination to keep the enemy at bay was etched on every face.

Right: We don't know who this little chap is, but we do know when and where. The location is on the way to Hardcastle Crags above Hebden Bridge. The date is sometime in the early years of the Second World War, most probably early 1940. The little lad may look quite at home, but records say he was not from Hebden Bridge but an evacuee from one of our larger centres. At the start of the

Second World War in 1939 German bombing was expected to quickly devastate cities such as London and Leeds, Liverpool and Manchester. In response to that threat the Government arranged for many thousands of children to be evacuated, sent to safety, to live with families in more rural parts of Britain. This young chap is one of them. Not every household forced to have strange children billeted on them was happy with the arrangement; and many evacuees had horror stories to tell. But this evacuee at least looks happy enough with a hoop to play with. The young fellow is wearing clogs, still at that time familiar everyday footwear for many people. Though evacuation had begun in September, 1939, there were, initially, none of the feared German bomber raids. By Christmas many children had been reclaimed and returned home. Between 7 September, 1940, and 10 May, 1941, however the 'Blitz' hit many towns and cities across the country, it began with the bombing of London. By the end of May, 1941, bombing had killed over 43,000 civilians.

Left and below: The back streets of Halifax typified every other one across the land on 8 May, 1945. Victory in Europe was assured and it was time to have a shindig. There was still work to be done in the Far East, but at least the threat nearer to home had been removed. The sailor, home from the sea in this photograph, was very popular with both old and young as he represented all the brave boys who had risked everything on land, sea and air in defence of our realm. One woman found a piano accordion and played a fine hokey-cokey on it so that her neighbours could enjoy an old-fashioned knees-up. Before long, trestle tables were borrowed from church halls and schoolrooms. Out came the tablecloth from the bottom drawer in the sideboard and dining room and kitchen chairs were dragged out into the street. It was party time. Margarine was spread on the sandwiches and every last ration coupon went to make this a day to remember. All at once the drab years were forgotten and, for now, the shortages no longer mattered. But it was not all unbridled joy. Some women shed a quiet tear for the sweetheart or father who would not be coming home. For each one who looked forward to the day when she would be reunited with her husband, there was another who knew that hers lay in a foreign field. Lest we forget.

Below: Brighouse town centre was festooned with flags, bunting and streamers on VE Day. Marching bands struck up with their rousing marches and cheering crowds lined the streets as the good news that the war was over was relayed to every home in the land. For six long years, ever since the Nazi tanks rolled into Poland on the first day of September in 1939, we Britons had fretted about the future. Would our little island survive the onslaught from the enemy and would little Jimmy really sleep in his own bed again? Now we knew that the threat had gone and that he was safe and the bluebirds could be released across those white cliffs. Although formal celebrations were held and fine words spoken from the Town Hall steps, it was the collective relief felt by those in the crowd that seemed to dominate. We had been winning the war of late, according to newsreel reports and newspaper stories about the Allied push across Germany and towards Berlin, but there had been false dawns before and the more pragmatic amongst us knew all about propaganda. But, now it was official. Germany had surrendered, so let the party begin.

Above: The cost of fighting the war was huge, and year by year massive fund-raising campaigns were staged in towns and cities across Britain to persuade people to invest in bonds and certificates. Parades were always a feature, and this photograph of 1940 shows Red Cross nurses and the St John Ambulance Brigade winding their way along Cow Green and turning smartly left at the old Crown and Anchor at Bull Green. This may well have been associated with War Weapons Week, which also had weapons exhibitions, parades by the Duke of Wellington's Regiment, bomb disposal demonstrations and a schools' poster competition. The aim for Halifax was to raise at least £1 million, enough for three destroyers. The big inducement also was that the money was being lent to the government, not given, and even a £5 bond would pay for a five inch shell. Halifax War Weapons Week raised £2,562,939, or the staggering sum of over £26 per head - a record for the country, until Elland beat it the following year.

ROYAL VISITS

D uring the 1949 royal visit of Princess Elizabeth, schoolchildren were given time off from their lessons so that they could demonstrate their support for the monarchy

and have the opportunity of seeing the future queen at close quarters when she stopped at Spring Hall. Pupils from Warley Road School cheered with gusto to let their royal visitor know how much they loved her. These little monkeys went a bit over the top for the sake of the photographer, but they enjoyed the occasion and were very sure that everyone around them knew how much fun they were having. When the 23-year-old Princess came past they waved little flags on sticks and hollered as loudly as they could. To see a celebrity in the flesh was something special. There was no television for these children, so they had only been able to get glimpses of members of the royal family through occasional newspaper photographs or clips on a newsreel at the cinema. To see a special person in close up was a treat indeed. The schoolchildren at Spring Hall, standing to attention as they honoured their visitors, could not be accused of neglecting their patriotic duties. John Haley, in his white, short sleeved shirt, was concentrating so hard on hitting the right notes that his eyes were closed in concentration. Next to him, in the long sleeved shirt, Rodney Wade belted out the words with gusto. It is good to look back some 60 years and see boys in short trousers and, in a couple of cases, socks at half mast standing next to girls in frocks, blouses and skirts. Thank goodness, too, for a teacher in a jacket, collar and tie rather than a pair of jeans and T-shirt.

Above: King George V and Queen Mary came here in 1912, just two years after his father Edward VII had died. This was a time when the royal heads of Europe were coming under pressure at parliamentary level, from the working classes and by the upper echelons of society as well. In other words, countries were in a state of flux as the old order came under pressure. Britain's powerful empire brought more affluence to the already rich, the Germans sought to expand their influence across the continent and the Russians sought to control the starving masses in their vast country. Coincidentally, George, Wilhelm and Nicholas, the respective heads of state, were all cousins, being grandchildren of Queen Victoria. Yet, by the end of this decade, the first would change his family name from Saxe-Coburg-Gotha to Windsor, the second would be in exile and the third butchered by revolutionaries. The royal couple had little idea of the turmoil that lay ahead as they posed for this formal portrait. Yet, the assassination of Arch Duke Franz Ferdinand in Sarajevo was just two years away and the horrors of the Great War and the uprising in Russia would soon follow.

Below: King George V and Queen Mary passed though Elland on their way from Halifax to Huddersfield on 11 July, 1912. It may have been just a fleeting visit, but the townspeople were not going to let the occasion pass by without displaying their sense of national pride and fidelity to the monarchy. Streets were decked out in glorious fashion, perhaps with bunting saved from the coronation celebrations the year before. People dressed up for the occasion, fishing out their Sunday best. The large lady on the right wore the same frock that she done the previous year, but the working classes did not have an extensive wardrobe and the dress would not be worn all that often and it had to last. The children scrubbed up well and looked very smart in all their finery. This would probably be their only chance of seeing this king and queen in the flesh and it was important that they looked their best. New Street had previously won a prize as being the best decorated street in Elland. It pulled out all the stops to repeat its victory and the effort was worthwhile when it retained its title. At the end of the day, the streamers and flags came down and were put away until they were needed again. That day would come in different circumstances when they marked Armistice Day in 1918.

Below: The Rock Tavern, on Dewsbury Road, at Upper Edge, Elland was the centre of the local community's celebrations for the Coronation Day of King George V on 22 June, 1911. The licensee, Harry Hodgson, played host as all the children in the village turned up, accompanied by a number of adults, to take part in a sheep roasting. If the source of food in question is the creature to the right of the photograph, then we can all say 'aagh' together. The kiddies were destined to have a great time, even if the forerunner of Shawn the Sheep was about to come to a gruesome end. It was less than a decade earlier that the country rejoiced in honour of a new king, Edward VII, but that was before many of these little ones were born. Edward died in 1910 and was succeeded by his second son. The male who should have been the heir apparent, Prince Albert, died from influenza in 1892. At the time, he was engaged to Princess Mary of Teck. George replaced his brother both in the line of succession to the throne and at the altar, for he married Mary in 1893. In later life she was renowned for some of the striking headpieces that she wore, with colourful toques being among the most memorable.

Facing page: Halifax was honoured by a royal visit in 1937 when King George VI and Queen Elizabeth came to see us and visit Shibden Hall. Despite being the consort, it was the former

Elizabeth Bowes-Lyon who took the lead in this photograph, much as she did in life. Although he was the head of state, she was a definite driving force behind the throne. Born in 1900 to the future Earl of Strathmore, Elizabeth was a remarkable beauty and doyenne of the minor Scottish aristocracy, a young woman who was very popular in the gatherings of the rich and well born on the London society scene. She was not short of suitors and it came as no surprise when 'Bertie', the young Prince Albert and Duke of York, proposed to her in 1921. However, Elizabeth turned him down as she was fearful of having her free spirit shackled by the pressures and constraints of becoming part of the Windsor household. When Albert told his mother, Queen Mary, that he would marry no other, she went to Glamis and visited the woman who had stolen her son's heart. She, too, was convinced that this was the one for him. With the backing of his parents, Albert proposed several times more and, eventually, Elizabeth accepted. The couple became engaged in January, 1923, and were married three months later. Albert took the name 'George' when he acceded to the throne in 1936. King George VI was something of a reluctant King. Fortunately, he had a wife at his side who was able to help him perform the duties of a monarch that he found difficulty to carry out. In the 1920s, she became known as 'the

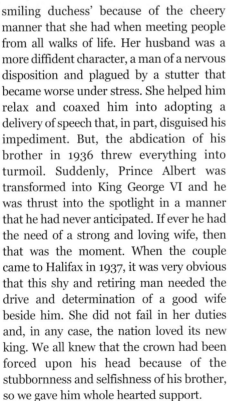

smiling duchess' because of the cheery manner that she had when meeting people from all walks of life. Her husband was a more diffident character, a man of a nervous disposition and plagued by a stutter that became worse under stress. She helped him relax and coaxed him into adopting a delivery of speech that, in part, disguised his impediment. But, the abdication of his brother in 1936 threw everything into turmoil. Suddenly, Prince Albert was transformed into King George VI and he was thrust into the spotlight in a manner that he had never anticipated. If ever he had the need of a strong and loving wife, then that was the moment. When the couple came to Halifax in 1937, it was very obvious that this shy and retiring man needed the drive and determination of a good wife beside him. She did not fail in her duties and, in any case, the nation loved its new king. We all knew that the crown had been forced upon his head because of the stubbornness and selfishness of his brother, so we gave him whole hearted support.

Far Right: On 29 July, 1949, the country was struggling to get back on its feet after the war. The austerity of the period was difficult for Britons to accept. Let us face it, we had won the war, but what had we to show for it? This was the way that most of us felt. Rationing was still in force and there were shortages everywhere. Europe was still a mess and we were in debt to the Americans for what seemed like ever more. The spectre of communism raised its ugly head and the worries of another, more devastating war was not far from everybody's minds as more and more powerful nuclear weapons were on the horizon. We needed something to lift our spirits during this time of doom and gloom. What better than a royal visit for that little bit of joy? We could celebrate, just for a while, something that marked us out from many other countries. Most of them had presidents, but we had a proper king and queen. Their daughter, Princess Elizabeth, accompanied by her husband, Prince Philip, rode in an open topped limousine through Elland. Locals turned out en masse to cheer the couple and enjoy a moment when they could forget their woes and celebrate being British.

Below: Princess Elizabeth visited the Reflecting Roadstud factory during her 1949 tour of Calderdale. Standing behind her on the far left is the man who helped revolutionise road safety in the 1930s with an invention that, with certain modifications, is still widely used three quarters of a century after its conception. Percy Shaw (1890-1976) was born at Lee Mount, before moving as a toddler to Boothtown, where he would spend the rest of his

life. One version of history has him driving home at night along an unlit road, when his headlights picked out a cat at the edge of the roadside and he saw the lights reflected in the creature's eyes. On arriving home, he thought about the experience and how the cast's eyes had helped identify the edge of the road. An industry was born. He began experimenting with designs and, in 1935, set up his company to manufacture reflective road studs that could be used in different positions on a highway to mark out its centre or edge. A patent was granted the following year. Shaw was not the only inventor working on road studs, but his were the best. The reflective lenses were forced into a rubber housing when a wheel passed over them and then popped out again in a self-cleaning action. The cat's eye nickname stuck and the widespread adoption of Shaw's invention must have saved many thousands of lives on our roads during the wartime blackout and the years since.

Bottom right: One of Todmorden's best-loved sons, Geoff Love, is seen here in the late 1970s being presented to the Queen at the Royal Albert Hall, before the Royal Film

Harmonic performance –a celebration of music from films – arranged and conducted by Geoff. He was born in 1917, in Todmorden, and died in1991: Geoff was nationally famous as an easy-listening orchestra leader and made many recordings of his own as well as alongside other stars such as Shirley Bassey. His father was an American-born guitarist and dancer and his mother an actress. As a child in Todmorden he began to learn to play the violin but then switched to the trombone. He embarked on a solo musical career before military service during the Second World War in the King's Royal Rifle Corps. In 1955 Geoff Love formed his own band for the television show On the Town, and went on to make numerous recordings. His first hit was a cha-cha-cha, Patricia, in 1948. He was a constant presence on radio and television as a personality, composer, musical director, arranger, accompanist and, from 1959, as 'Manuel and his Music of the Mountains'. In this guise Geoff released many records. During the 1970s he appeared with singer Max Bygraves in the Thames Television music show SingalongaMax. Geoff returned to his Yorkshire roots in the late 1980s. He became involved with various brass band traditions, participated in the Saddleworth Whit Friday contest and played with the local band in annual concerts at Todmorden Town Hall.

AROUND THE SHOPS

Everyone was well guarded against the elements on Southgate as this damp, overcast day in 1962 made sure that raincoats and brollies were necessary rather than fashion items. Those crossing the street from the Albany Arcade towards Tailorfit kept a wary eye out for the traffic, even though they were on a zebra crossing. The town was becoming quite congested with the increase in car ownership that reflected the more comfortable living standards that we were now experiencing. Unemployment was low and the majority of shoppers on view had money in their pockets and purses. The shop tills rang out regularly as customers spent their cash in some of the retail outlets we can see on the left. Hutchison's was the place to come for your packet of cigarettes. Pipe smokers enjoyed sampling some of the fine, aromatic tobaccos that were on sale and those who liked a good cigar could roll a fine Havana between their fingers before parting with their money. Jessops was one of a number of tailors in the vicinity and, if shopping was too much of an effort, you could always pop into the café next door for a refreshing cuppa. The scene is little changed today, with the exception of the traffic jams. Warren James' jewellers, Priceless shoes and Game are the names on the shop fronts, but the buildings are otherwise the same.

Left: The Borough Market is still thriving over a century since it first opened its doors to traders and the general public. Building work began in late 1891 and the foundation stone laid in October 1892, but the market was still a year from completion when this photograph was taken in 1895. The final cost of building was £130,000. On 25 July, 1896, the Duke and Duchess of York, the future King George V and Queen Mary, presided at the official opening ceremony. Rental of a shop in the market cost anything from £13 to £36 per annum, depending upon floor space. The individual stalls were rented out weekly and cost the traders half a crown (12.5p), for the most humble pitch, or eight shillings (40p) for the best spot. The shops in the Arcades were for an even better class of merchant and they set back their tenants a right royal £100 per year. Because of its grand architecture and importance as a feature in the town's heritage, the market is a Grade II listed building. In 2008 it won an award for being the best market hall in the country.

Below: Traffic along Southgate is restricted now, as it is in other parts of town, but well over half a century ago cars and buses moved happily along the street. Parking was

SOUTHGATE HALIFAX.

permitted and, this will shock younger readers, it was free! The photograph was taken at the corner with King Edward Street. Looking towards Cornmarket, the small truck in the centre of the road was turning into Cheapside and, away in the distance, we can make out the distinctive shape of the Burton tailoring store on the corner with Old Market. Montague Burton (1885-1952) was a Lithuanian Jew who came to England at the start of the last century. Born Moshe Osinsky, he opened a tailor's in Chesterfield in 1903, using the name of a nearby town as his business name. Although he called himself by the title by which he became famous, Burton did not legally change his name until much later. This caused him problems in the First World War as he was often accused of being some form of spy or even traitor. His rise to fame as the 'tailor of taste' is a real tale of rags to riches. By the 1930s nearly every town in England had a Burton's on its High Street, many built to a similar design.

Above: With Coronation Street off to the left, Southgate in Elland is pictured as it looked in about 1935. Until 1910, the Post Office occupied the premises opposite the Royal George that are here home to the Liverpool Stores that moved from 22 Westgate. Central Bazaar, where H Littlewood once traded, occupies 39 Southgate. The advert for Brooke Bond tea was a simple statement, without a single chimpanzee in sight. We had our advertising gimmicks and slogans, even during the interwar years, but it was television advertising that advanced the use of jingles and catchy sayings so that some of them became part of our everyday language. Elland is a busy place, just as it was over 70 years ago. As a compact area, space is at a premium and nowadays motorists take great care as they are never sure that a shopper is not about to jump out and off the pavement in front of the car. Nearby Coronation Street is home to something of an anachronism in this day and age. The Rex Cinema continues to operate as a little independent outlet. Its Thursday morning cut price shows for pensioners are a wonderful throwback in time. A light swings overhead when the draught takes it and the organ plays as free cuppas are served before the show. As the trailers are shown, a woman wanders up the aisles calling out, 'Let's 'ave yer 'olders' as she collects the used cups in a large black binbag. Perfection.

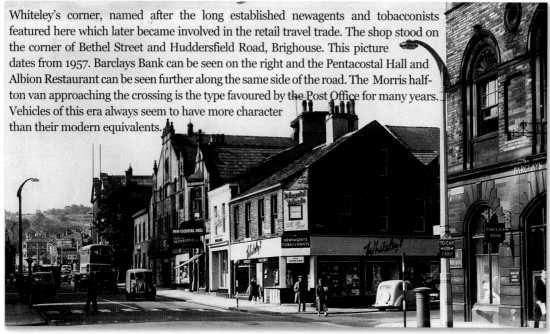

Whiteley's corner, named after the long established newagents and tobacconists featured here which later became involved in the retail travel trade. The shop stood on the corner of Bethel Street and Huddersfield Road, Brighouse. This picture dates from 1957. Barclays Bank can be seen on the right and the Pentacostal Hall and Albion Restaurant can be seen further along the same side of the road. The Morris half-ton van approaching the crossing is the type favoured by the Post Office for many years. Vehicles of this era always seem to have more character than their modern equivalents.

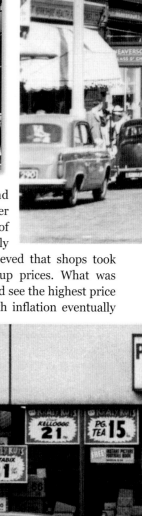

Opposite right: Gazing down Russell Street from Cornmarket towards Market Street in the 1950s saw Halliday's and Halford's on the opposite corner, where WH Smith stands today. On the left hand side of Russell Street, Pinders and Taylor's chemist shop have changed hands, but Neaverson's is still in situ at No 5 and in the Old Arcade. With its delightful display of glass, china and other collectables, this business has over a century of tradition behind it in the very same handsome premises. Some famous names that pop up on TV's 'Bargain Hunt', such as Moorcroft, can be found in Neaverson's impressive cabinets. Will JJB Sports, at the right hand end of Russell Street still be there in the 22nd century? The shop on the far right, where a Burton's branch stands now, belonged to Timothy Whites and Taylors. For many years, this was the main rival to Boots on Britain's high streets, especially in the south of England where it was founded. The Nottingham based company won the day in 1968 when its financial muscle was too great and Boots took it over in a coup that removed its chief competitor from the scene. The cameraman in this photograph had his back to the former Marks & Spencer building, currently used by the Wilkinson store.

Right: 'Krazy Kuts', the Co-op supermarket in Dale Street, Todmorden, was captured by the camera in 1970. The prices in the windows are all displayed in 'real money'. On Monday, 15 February, 1971, however, Britain went decimal. Real money - pounds, shillings and pence - was replaced by a novel system with 100 pence in the pound rather than 240. Shillings, florins half-crowns and tanners passed into history. For a short time the old and the new money ran hand in hand. Shoppers could pay in pounds, shillings and pence and get 'new pence' in their change. The idea was to keep the old money in circulation for up to eighteen months. In the end the old penny, halfpenny and threepenny bit ceased to be legal tender in August, 1971. For a while a handful of shops refused to switch, but inevitably even they had to change. Many believed that shops took advantage of the confusion to put up prices. What was certainly true was that the 1970s would see the highest price rises ever experienced in Britain, with inflation eventually

peaking at close to 30 per cent. The ironically named 'Krazy Kuts', Todmorden's first food supermarket, was built in 1967 to replace the fire-damaged section of the old Co-op building. All the remaining branches of the once independent Todmorden Co-op were by then owned by the Rochdale Co-op. In 1970 'Krazy Kuts' was a state of the art shopping experience. Within a year or two the 'Lion' supermarket opened in Bridge Street providing fierce competition.

Below: This is 'shoe shop street', as it became known to locals for obvious reasons when you look on the right and immediately spot True Form and Timpsons. Crown Street is somewhat changed now, with Dolland and Aitchison on the corner instead of Gledhills and Holland and Barrett and Bet Fred replacing the shoe shops. The view up and away from the town centre, across Cow Green, is now obliterated by high rise development and a multi-storey car park. Taken in 1962, the photograph shows a young woman of Afro Caribbean race on the left. It was not yet a common occurrence to see anything other than white faces on our streets. There had been

some immigration after World War II, especially from the West Indies, but stringent laws restricted many from bringing families over later on. People from the former Asian colonies arrived in large numbers in the 1960s and 1970s following the passing of the 1962 Commonwealth Immigrants Act. The ranks were swelled by Idi Amin's persecution of Ugandan Asians in 1972. Immigration was curbed once again by further Acts of Parliament in the mid 1970s. Nowadays, most towns and cities have a variety of families who have origins from across the globe. In the township of Halifax, some 10 per cent of residents have links with Asia.

Above: In the 1970s, it was possible to look down the Woolshops and clearly see the parish church across and beyond Square Road. At that time, Modelle Fashions occupied the site where WH Smith holds sway today. Below it was Jeffrey's bedding shop, a fairly short lived enterprise. On the opposite corner, KM Lent sold household furnishings and Arthur Ellis traded in kitchen appliances. Somewhat remarkably, this latter shop was still selling wringers, surely something of an anachronism even as long ago as 1970. The Woolshops are close to the Piece Hall and take us back to the time when local weavers produced worsted in the area that led to the creation of the famous Hall and the prosperity of the merchants that grew as trade increased. Daniel Defoe, the author and chronicler, visited Halifax in 1724. Even then, half a century before the Piece Hall was built, he noted that 'their business is the clothing trade and each clothier must keep a horse or two to fetch home his wool and carry his yarn to the spinners'.

AT LEISURE

Below: Gibson Mill sits in the heart of Hardcastle Crags, the area of beautiful woodland, punctuated by stacks formed of millstone grit. It was built at the start of the 19th century as a water powered spinning mill and was one of the first generation of its type that operated during the industrial revolution. By 1833, it had 21 employees producing cotton cloth and they put in an average working week of 72 hours. It closed down in around 1890, but returned to life a decade or so later as an 'entertainment emporium'. There was a dining room, dance hall, roller skating rink, tea kiosks and boating on the mill pond. It fell into disuse in the 1940s and was left to the National Trust in 1956 by Abraham Gibson, of Greenwood Lee. Lord Holme Mill is its real name, but that is seldom used. In the early 2000s, extensive renovations to the mill and its cottages were carried out to turn the site into a visitor and education centre. Those coming here can now enjoy exhibitions about the mill's industrial past and the leisure uses to which it was put in later years, as well as taking in the natural charms of Hardcastle Crags.

Right: The appearance of a helter skelter at Todmorden market provides an entertaining distraction for local folk, as well as being a fine subject for local amateur photographer Willie Eastwood who captured this scene in 1906. Because of the long exposure of the photographic plate necessary in those days those subjects who have moved during the process appear almost ghostly. Though none can now be alive who paid a penny to ride the helter skelter on this day long ago, the picture will still revive memories of other, later rides. Who could possibly forget? Do you recall the heroic effort needed by small hands to lift one of the strange smelling, heavy coconut-hair mats up the steep stairs to the top? Of being out of breath and full of anticipation on the way up? The darkness inside the tower and the cracks of light shining through the tall, wooden structure? The spiral staircase seemed never ending. The sudden emergence into daylight and the careful positioning of the mat on the slide before letting go to who knew what. The ride, of course, was over all too soon – unless the final moment was marred by that perennial risk of friction burns from the long matting at the end. As for more serious folk, 1906 was an election year and party manifestos had been scrupulously examined. The result was a major victory for the Liberal Party with 399 seats. The Conservatives collected just 156 with the fledgling Labour Party managing just 29. Even the Irish Nationalist eclipsed Labour, gaining 82 seats.

Above: Perhaps Enid Blyton could have used this scene as an inspiration for a new series of books. If she had, then instead of the Famous Five or Secret Seven, there might have been the Tremendous Ten. The nine children, along with Mick the dog, were having a whale of a time on the see-saw, precariously perched on several blocks of stone. No doubt their mums had warned them that it would all end in tears, but youngsters need to take a few risks and experience the odd scraped knee in order to mature. They need to be protected, but not cosseted. From the left, Sarah Wadsworth, Margaret Gill, Mary and Richard Greenwood, Geoff Sunderland, Alice Marsland, Sarah Greenwood, Winnie Holt and Ida Sunderland had a lovely time playing at the north end of Church Street, Heptonstall, in 1921. So what, if they came down to earth with a bump as they could dust themselves off and start all over again.

Top right, facing page: Happy days! The children's paddling pool at Centre Vale Park Todmorden, was built in the mid-1920s. Its construction followed the completion of the Garden of Remembrance, the tennis courts and three more bowling greens. Visitors to the park had even more to enjoy when a nine-hole miniature golf course opened in 1938. Few childhood memories can surely be complete without those of splashing around in a paddling pool on a hot summer's afternoon – not least in those times when holidays away from home were a rarity for most, and often meant holidaying at home rather than a visit to the seaside. Even in the colder weather of winter the pool provided entertainment in a different way, being the ideal venue for model yachting. Thousands of boys, and not a few girls will have indelible memories of launching toy yachts from one side of the pool before racing around the water in the confident expectation – not always met - that the wind would blow the vessel safely to the other side. Time took its inevitable toll of the original paddling pool. By the 1960s, forty years after this happy scene was captured for posterity, the pool had lost much of its attraction. The polio scares in the 1950s led to many paddling pools being permanently drained, By then the pool had also become surrounded by trees and shrubbery inevitably leading to cracks in its structure: as a consequence it was eventually relocated within the children's playground in the park.

Right: A somewhat informal example of maypole dancing taking place in Adelaide Street, Todmorden, in May, 1960. Though half the folk around today seem to imagine that the May Day bank holiday has something to do with celebrating the Russian Revolution, or perhaps the birth of Karl Marx, nothing could be further from the truth. May Day is an ancient pagan fertility festival, later co-opted and tolerated by the Christian

the 20th century! Maypole dancing took place in most neighbourhoods each year on 1 May, with a May Queen being chosen from among local girls. And what excitement and jealously that could raise, with mothers convinced beyond reason that their disappointed daughters were the ones that really had the strongest claim to the throne. The overt symbolism, obvious in previous centuries, was long lost by the 20th century to be replaced by a gentle and civilised folk custom which delighted everyone involved in the annual celebrations. Sadly, this tradition seems to have largely died out as a fixed event in the public calendar, although the practice still continues intermittently. Elsewhere in

church. Some say that once upon a time the May Queen was sacrificed at the end of the festivities – though if true there are certainly no recorded instances of such an event in Calderdale in

Calderdale the fact that maypole dancing was once quite literally a central part of village life is commemorated in the name of the Maypole Inn at Warley in the heart of the village.

Right: Dating from the late 1930s this scene will bring back memories, not just for those who were children in that hungry decade, but also for those who were young for many decades afterwards. The classic 'witch's hat' roundabout was a feature of children's playgrounds until the 1970s, when the design fell foul of elf 'n' safety officials who deemed them too dangerous for youngsters to play on. Well maybe the were a little bit dangerous, but they were certainly fun: get a gang of big boys all round, and the entire thing could be lifted off its mounting. And of course the witch's hat didn't just go round and round – the design meant it could swing at same time. True, some children did lose a few teeth as a consequence of getting too close. This particular photo appears to have been taken at Spring Edge, King Cross.

Below: Brighouse has been promised new swimming baths for years, though those plans never seem to get any nearer. Even in the 1950s when this photograph was taken there must have been calls for a replacement. Though the exact circumstances of this occasion are lost in the mists of time, it seems probable that it was a schools event since the man with the receding hairline sat on the left is believed to be Mr L C Jones the headmaster of St Martin's Secondary School. Public baths were rather different in the 1950s than they are today. The idea of them as all-purpose 'leisure centres' was certainly in no one's mind when they were first built. In the days when very few homes had bathrooms, many with not even running water, public baths were built which didn't simply provide public swimming pools but equally, and perhaps more importantly, bathrooms were one could have a hot soak in a bath tub, paying a few pennies for a small bar of soap and the rent of a towel. The first of Britain's public baths and washhouses opened in Liverpool in 1842. How times have changed.Meanwhile, what memories this scene must evoke amongst the thousands of readers who once participated in such events themselves. Were you a water babe will medals galore and who won every race, or perhaps one of the less happy swimmers who gloried only in that first proficiency certificate for managing to swim just a single length of the pool?

Left: John Wilson, a fabrics manufacturer, founded Forest Mill at Ovenden in 1818. He also built several villas and Forest Cottage for his family members. The community centre on Cousin Lane takes its name from there. Ovenden Youth Club, seen here at the Forest Cottage Centre, was one of the many similar places that young people went to in the 1950s and 1960s. There they could have a game of darts or table tennis and play pop music on 78s and the later 45s as they just listened to young Elvis or danced around to the wild sounds of Little Richard. When youngsters went to such clubs they made sure that they were appropriately dressed. The girls starched their swirling petticoats and ironed their dresses, while the boys Brylcreemed their hair and put on their smart shirts and natty ties. They never complained that there was nowhere to go or that they had nothing to do. Teenagers, the newly coined description, knew how to entertain themselves and be entertained. Alderman Dryden Brook MP was the guest of honour on this occasion. He became the Member of Parliament for Halifax in 1945 in the Labour landslide and served until 1955 when he lost his seat to Maurice Macmillan, son of the future prime minister.

Above: It's the bleak mid-winter at the Shay, the grimness of the day being enhanced by bristling mill chimneys and the barren wastes of Southowram Bank in the background. What a forbidding sight for any visiting team! Cold it might have been, but plenty of heat and excitement was being generated in the ground, for although the exact date of this photograph is unknown, it is likely to have been taken during the FA Cup Fifth Round tie between Halifax Town and Tottenham Hotspur in 1953. The game was played on a snow-covered pitch in front of a massive crowd of 36,885. Such details fit the bill very well, along with the fact that the illustrious Spurs team, containing such great names as Alf Ramsey and Bill Nicholson, played in white shirts and black shorts. Town had a useful outfit in 1953, one that had already disposed of first division opponents Cardiff City and Stoke City in previous rounds of the cup. Long-standing Town supporters will well remember the half-back line of Geddes, Packard and Moss, with goal scorers such as Darbyshire and Priestley up front. Town met their match that day, however, as the powerful North London team ended up as 3-0 winners. Halifax Town supporters have been a long-suffering bunch, and there have been more 'downs' than 'ups' since the club's debut game in the old Third Division North in 1921. Nevertheless, those who were there will

Halifax Dukes, (back row): Bert Kingston, Bob Jamieson, Reg Fearman (promoter), Ray Day, Bryan Elliott, (front row): Dave Younghusband, Eric Boocock and Eric Boothroyd.

Images courtesy of: www.defunctspeedway.co.uk

still feel a warm glow at the memory of that Watney Cup victory over Manchester United - Best, Law, Charlton and all - in 1971!

Above and right: The lure of the smell of burning rubber, the taste of the cinder track in the back of your throat and the roar of the bikes has always been difficult to refuse. In 1929, the sport was still in its infancy and only a limited number of events were held at Thrum Hall. There were races on public roads and on large racetracks, such as Brooklands and Goodwood, but smaller, self-contained ones that often doubled as dog tracks or shared premises with rugby clubs were still being developed. However, it was not until the late 1940s that the sport took off in a really big way. Halifax Nomads raced briefly, before Halifax Dukes came along. Named for the Duke of Wellington's Regiment, the club enjoyed the reception from a crowd of 18,000 for its inaugural fixture at the Shay in 1949. Unfortunately, the bubble burst quite quickly and the Dukes folded in 1951. Speedway did not return to the Shay until 1965, but it came back with something of a bang and, before long, was attracting crowds larger than the soccer team could bring in. Speedway stayed here until 1985 when disagreement between the two sports over finances prompted the Dukes to move to Bradford.

a while, the alley flourished, but later became a cut price supermarket. The sport has been revived in latter years by the opening of a new bowl on the far end of Commercial Street.

Right: Now, there's posh. This photograph was taken on 23 December, 1949. Goodness, most people could not afford a radiogram, never mind a television back then. It would not be long, though, before this luxury became an essential part of family entertainment. Until then, an invitation to watch a programme on someone's private set was a privilege. It was the 1953 Coronation and that year's FA Cup Final that helped promote the invasion of the goggle box into all our lives. When those events occurred, people with TVs suddenly discovered that they were the most popular neighbours in the street as locals with whom they had seldom shared a conversation were able to negotiate an invite into the front room. After enjoying the entertainment offered by the splendour of the wedding coach on its way to Westminster Abbey and a seven goal thriller at Wembley, dads were instructed to put television high on the list of goods that they could get on hire purchase. To modern youth the tiny screens and fuzzy pictures would seem hilarious. But, to those of us who were around at the time, it was a magical experience. The kids had Muffin the Mule, Andy Pandy and The Flowerpot Men. Adults watched panel games like 'What's My Line' and exciting drama such as 'The Quatermass Experiment' until the little white dot on the screen faded.

Far right: Larger-than-life figure 'Big Daddy' ranked among the country's wrestling legends and arguably the most popular wrestler in British history. The man known to us as 'Big Daddy' was born in the Wilson Street area of Halifax, as Shirley Crabtree Jnr on November 14, 1930. According to some accounts, his grandmother picked "Shirley" from a novel by the

Above: Although the roadway has been modified in more recent times to include traffic lights, a subway and a different angle of junction where the roundabout stood, this elevated view of the Broad Street intersection with Orange Street and Waterhouse Street is still very recognisable. Some of the establishments we can see are a sign of the changing times. On the left, the Brunswick Bowling Alley did good trade for a while. The 10 pin boom of the early 1960s was assisted by some television exposure on ITV's 'World of Sport', but it was not the most gripping of action to captivate Saturday afternoon audiences. For

Giant Haystacks watched by 'World of Sport' audiences in excess of 10 million. His 'bad guy' opponents like Mick McManus had to put up with a barrage of abuse from normally mild mannered and softly spoken "grannies". Famously he would also be noted for being the first wrestler to remove the mask from Kendo Nagasaki during a televised match, but this proved a big anti-climax as the mystical character was revealed as an ordinary looking English man. It was said at the time that among his many fans was Queen Elizabeth and then Prime Minister, Margaret Thatcher.

Fans always felt reassured that regardless of how the bout was going, 'Big Daddy' could always rely on the famous "belly-splash" to get the better of his opponents and this was often met with the chants of "Easy, Easy" from the crowd.

same name by Charlotte Bronte for his father, who was a part time pro-wrestler before him.

As countless generations before him he started his working life as a coal miner in a local pit, but he was never fully commited. He also played rugby league for Bradford Northern, but never made a first team appearance. Whilst working as a lifeguard at a local swimming pool, Shirley's fascination with body building and wrestling grew. Aged 16, Shirley was introduced to wrestling legend George Hackenschmidt, who started to train him in the art of wrestling. Eventually he found his way into life as a professional wrestler in 1952. Over the early years using such ring names as 'The Blond Adonis', 'Mr Universe and the 'The Battling Guardsman'. During this period he won two British Federation titles before he quit out of frustration and retired from top level competition. During this period he teamed up with his brother Max, who was just starting in the wrestling business as a promoter, and formed his own "carnival sideshow" promotion out of Blackpool. The bigger shows they ran were often opened by big name musical acts like Donovan and contained one of, if not the first female wrestling bouts, featuring Jenny Muff from Halifax.

It wasn't until 1976 that 'Big Daddy' was first given life in the ring by Crabtree, based on the Burl Ives Character in the 1958 screen adaptation of Tennessee Williams' Cat on a Hot Tin Roof. He invariably strode into the ring wearing his trademark Union flag jacket and spangled top hat. In his prime he weighed in at a hefty 26 stone with a massive 64 inch chest that had earned him a place in the Guinness Book of Records. Known originally for wearing a leotard emblazoned with just a large "D", he was hugely popular with people of all ages. He played the "good guy" in bouts against the likes of

On 1 June, 1969, the Flying Scotsman pulled a trainspotters' 'special' travelling to Newcastle via Bradford, Halifax and Carlisle. The locomotive's brief appearance in the Calder Valley was snapped by crowds of photographers lining the route, including David Tempest who took this picture taken from behind the Spinners Rest pub, on Knowlwood Road, Todmorden. The engine was built in 1923 by the LNER and represented the company at the British Empire Exhibition at Wembley in 1924. It was one of five engines selected to haul the prestigious non-stop Flying Scotsman train service from London to Edinburgh, hauling the first train on 1 May, 1928, along the 392-miles non-stop route in eight hours. On 30 November, 1934, the Flying Scotsman became the first steam locomotive to be officially recorded travelling at 100 mph. The rather less prestigious line through Calderdale rarely saw such majestic machines in normal service. But that hardly mattered, the engines we once did have were glorious enough in their own ways. Steam engines were wholly replaced by diesel locomotives by the late 1960s but could never be replaced in people's affection. The world was then much quieter, no jet engines screaming overhead and no roar from streams of traffic hurtling along six lane motorways. And the world was darker too, without modern sodium street lighting. A steam locomotive was the most powerful and fastest things most people would ever see. And one of the most visually impressive - not least at night roaring through the valley, snorting steam, smoke and sparks into the darkness.

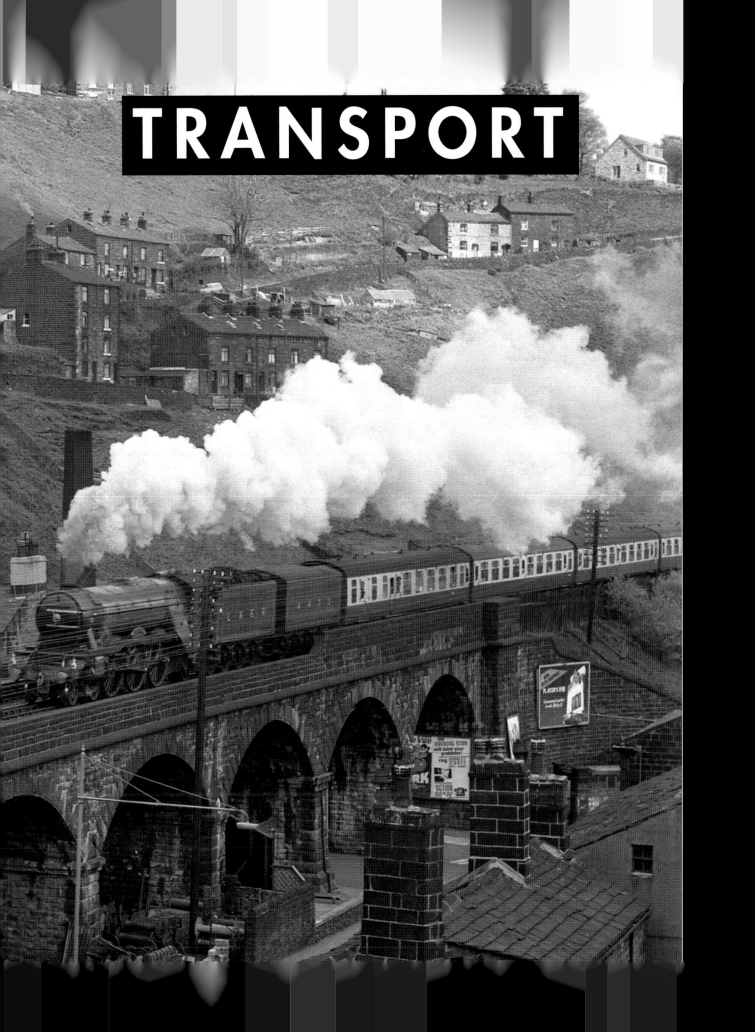

TRANSPORT

Left: This boneshaker of a motor car must have been one of the earliest ever seen in Calderdale. Amazingly, the cows in the field have taken it all in their stride. You would have thought the shock of seeing such a novel form of transport would have been enough to curdle the milk. The young man at the controls looks a little nervous as he clutches the horn, ready to warn unwary cyclists and pedestrians of his imminent arrival. Do you think that one of the smartly dressed women is his young lady and the other her chaperone, or is he merely the chauffeur? This very early car had a tiller instead of a steering wheel and was notoriously difficult to control. The steering wheel was not introduced until nearly 1900, though by the end of the Edwardian era all

new cars had dispensed with tillers. Speed limits in towns were very restrictive. On 28 January, 1896, Walter Arnold, of East Peckham, Kent became the first person in Great Britain to be successfully charged with speeding. Travelling at approximately 8 mph, he had exceeded the 2 mph speed limit for towns and was fined a shilling (5p) plus costs. Arnold had been caught by a policeman who had chased him down at breakneck speed on his bicycle. Out in the countryside, there were few restrictions and drivers could behave like Mr Toad as they whizzed along.

Left: The motor bus undertaking was beset by problems during the early years of operation. Not the least of these were the frequent interruptions to service, caused by accidents and breakdowns due to mechanical failure. On this particular occasion the No 2 bus travelling past Stansfield bridge, Todmorden, on its way to the Town Hall, veered out of control and ran into the wall of Roomfield Chapel, after the steering collapsed. The incident took place on March 18, 1907, some three months after the service began. Driver William Nothard was commended for remaining at his post, although his comment at the time may have us believe a slightly different story when he said "I couldn't get out of the damn thing!" Identifiable amongst the onlookers, who are seemingly more interested in the camera than the actual crash, are the local butcher Sam Newell and roadsweeper Albert Heliwell.

Above: The bus to Hullen Edge waited at its Halifax terminus as passengers got on board. Some might have had a little light refreshment in the White Horse, seen in the background at 33 Southgate. This was public transport in the early 1930s and meant that shoppers from the outlying towns and villages could access Halifax in a way that was not possible when their parents wanted to make the trip. For them, the pull up Salterhebble Hill was enough to test the fitness of the best of walkers and, in any case, it was at least a six mile round trip with Elland town centre just down the road. Even a journey by pony and trap would have had the poor old nag puffing and blowing from its exertions. Hullen Edge is home to both Elland's cricket and golf clubs and from both these places a fielder in the deep or a hacker on the fairway can enjoy fine views across the Black Brook valley and up the hillside towards Blackley.

Above and below: Goods trains ran right into Shaw's Mill, Holywell Green, in order to make deliveries and collect manufactured materials to take them away on their return journeys. Mill owners were very thankful for the service provided. In the days before rail, canal and road transport was painfully slow. As the industrial revolution saw great advances in the mechanisation of factories and manufacturing centres, production was restricted to the volume that could be moved on to outside markets. The coming of the railway meant that capacity could be greatly enlarged and, not surprisingly, many owners of industrial plants contributed to the creation of new tracks that they could access with ease. The Lancashire and Yorkshire Railway (L and YR) fully justified its nickname as 'the business line'. A major amalgamation with the East Lancashire Railway in 1859 meant that the L and YR could enjoy a near monopoly of trans-Pennine business throughout the rest of the century and into the next. The neckhold it had on Lancashire companies was completed in 1897 with the acquisition of the West Lancashire Railway. At its peak, just after the Great War, the L and YR owned 291 passenger stations on 601 route miles of track. On 1 January 1923, it was subsumed into the London, Midland and Scottish Railway. This was a government enforced move, following the Railways Act of 1921. During the war, the separate companies had come under state control in an effort to co-ordinate their business under the war effort. It

was found that many of the 120 companies were losing money and unable to reinvest to improve track and rolling stock. Lloyd George's government decided to move them away from internal competition in an attempt to keep some of the benefits of efficiency gained under its control in the preceding years. Complete nationalisation was considered and would eventually be imposed by the Attlee government under the 1947 Transport Act. In the meantime, a halfway house measure of grouping the railways within four large companies was introduced. The handsome 14 arch viaduct that stretches for 537 feet along its length at Holywell Green, seen across Rawroyds Lane, is a testament to the skill of Victorian engineers. A journey on a passenger train from Greetland had those on board marvelling at modern wonders of the world. A 13 arch viaduct carried the line for 690 feet over Saddleworth Road and Stainland Road and into West Vale Station, before moving on across this one as it headed towards the terminus.

Right: On the Friday night of September 4, 1942, a goods train left the rails at Todmorden viaduct and crashed down the embankment behind the market ground. With 28 coal wagons in tow, the train was heading towards Littleborough at 10pm when it was diverted into the loop line to allow another train to pass. In the loop line it overshot the buffers and plunged down the embankment, demolishing a telegraph pole in the process. The unfortunate driver was pinned between the engine and the tender for over two hours while a rescue party fought to dig him out from under the coal. This photograph shows the engine being craned back on to the rails ready to be taken away under for repair.

Below: Today's still-populsr cycle shop in King Cross is owned by Pedalsport the successor to the long-remembered Edgar Shaw, a business which had been inexistence since the 1940s. Here, however, is an even earlier incarnation of what is believed to be the same business, though then under the proprietorship of one S. Saville. Just as the Wright brothers of the same period seemed to think it perfectly natural to combine bicycle manufacture with building aeroplanes so, here in this picture, there seems nothing inherently odd about Mr Saville running his business as both a cycle shop and a car garage. Cars, however, were still just an interesting sideline, even in the 1920s. Very few folk could afford a motorcar, whilst to own a bicycle was an aspiration readily within the grasp of the far less affluent working classes. Curiously, the modern bicycle arrived almost exactly at the same point in history as the car, both benefiting from the invention of the pneumatic rubber tyre in 1888 and their mass-production in the 1890s. In 1885 John Kemp Starley, of Walthamstow, Essex, produced his Rover Safety Bicycle - a rear-wheel-drive, chain-driven cycle with two similar-sized wheels, far more stable than the 'penny-farthing'. Improved brakes, gears and other refinements led to a bicycle craze in Edwardian Britain. This enjoyable eco-friendly mode of transport would experience a second huge surge in popularity during the Great Depression of the 1930s as the cheapest form of transport available short of walking.

Facing page: At the height of its influence on the nation's transport system, the railways were everywhere, or so it seemed. Even villages had their own stations and many towns had more than one to serve passenger needs. Stainland Station was just another example of the way in which the tentacles of the rail network had spread out and into parts of rural Britain that had formerly to rely on horse drawn carts and carriages to get from place to place. The steam locomotive provided a revolution in many senses of the word. The stations that were built were not pokey affairs, but purpose built structures. Many had dedicated houses built for the stationmasters and their families. Stainland Station had its own porter's room and the Shaw family, waiting for their train, had no need to struggle with any bags that they might carry as there was a man always available to perform such duties. These passengers belonged to the family that helped with the cost of building this branch line. Other firms also contributed financial backing as it was originally opened as a goods line. In time, a passenger service was begun and three levels of service provided. Initially, the first class passengers paid the most, but travelled in carriages that were completely covered. Those with second class tickets had partial cover, but the third class passengers were out in the open. The earliest seating was on plain wooden benches, but these were later padded, though the depth of padding was dictated by the class of your carriage. Gas lighting was added in time to provide

additional comfort.The train standing at Holywell Green Station (above) was nicknamed 'the penny pusher'. It ran along the branch line to Greetland and thence into Halifax. The line continued to the left into the yard belonging to Shaw's Mill. The goods yard to the right was later occupied by Hoescht (UK) Ltd.

The branch line that terminated here was a short, double track one that served the local textile mills, providing them with coal and woollen yarn on one journey and taking back stone and worsted cloth on the return. Opened in 1875, it linked to the Sowerby Bridge-Wakefield line just east of Greetland. Even such a modest branch line attracted a large number of passengers and, by the time of its takeover by the London, Midland and Scottish Railway in 1923, some 16 trains per day were scheduled to use it. But, nothing lasts forever. Competition from the trams could not be overcome and commuters switched allegiances in increasing numbers. The passenger service was withdrawn in 1929, though freight continued to be carried for a further 30 years.

Above: The very first tram, or streetcar as the Americans like to call them, was run as a horse drawn transport system by the Swansea and Mumbles Railway Company in 1807. As the 19th century unfolded, steam power was used in many places, but the horse continued to be popular until the systems were electrified. Among the earliest ones using electricity was that developed by von Siemens in Berlin in 1881. The Halifax Corporation Tramways Act of 1897 paved the way for the introduction of an electric tramway system that was inaugurated on 9 June, 1898. The tram climbing the hill into Holywell Green in the early 1930s passed close by the Station Hotel. It was renamed the Holywell Inn in 1980 and, during refurbishment, a deep well was uncovered that was retained as a feature of the lounge bar. In much earlier times, the pub belonged to the Thornton family, of Ellistones Hall, in Stainland, before passing into the ownership of the Shaws, the owners of one of the large mills in the area.

Always a family to make sure that every opportunity to earn a penny was not overlooked, the Shaws distributed tokens to its workers that could be swapped for ale in their hostelry, thus ensuring that custom came their way rather than that of rival landlords.

Below left: The Cross Fields bus station was quite busy in 1968. It had been the central destination and departure point for Halifax since August, 1954. Long before there had been one on Wards End, opposite the Victoria Theatre, but it had proved to be unsuccessful. Before the war, the volume of buses on the roads was causing a logistical headache, especially along King Edward Street and Albion Street. They were so congested by public transport vehicles that they were of little use to any other form of traffic. The usual 'Something has to be done' cry went up, without any obvious answers. At last, general opinion was focused on providing a centralised bus station. Possible sites, such as Bull Green, George Street, Clare Road, Market Street and the Woolshops, were mooted. Of course, the balloon went up in 1939 and we all turned our attention to more pressing matters taking place across the English Channel. The present bus station is situated off Northgate. It was opened in 1989 by the MEP, Dr. Barry Seal, at a cost of £2 million. Incorporating part of the former Sion Congregational Chapel in its façade, it won an award as one of the North of England's most attractive modern buildings.

Above: In the 1960s when this photograph was taken Brighouse's bus station was located off Briggate. Buses had been running between Halifax and Brighouse since 1929. Today part this site to the right is occupied by the modern Wellington Arcade. In the background can be seen the spire of Brighouse's Central Methodist Church. These were of course the days when buses had conductors to not only take our fares but also to tell us to 'move on down please', as well as ring the bell to tell the driver to stop at the next bus stop. The always-cheerful chappies would help ladies burdened with bags, children and pushchairs. And they always had an extra smile when offered a half crown for a six-penny fare – they would gleefully be able to get rid of what seemed like a ton of copper change from their heavy moneybags! Until the 1970s the main road to Wakefield passed directly through the town centre of Brighouse, along Commercial Street, which as a consequence become a notorious traffic blackspot. In 1976 the Lunderscheild Link was opened. This short length of dual carriageway just north of the town centre, and parallel to Commercial Street, transformed the town centre and made it a far more shopper-friendly place. As part of the demolition and building works which went into the by-pass Brighouse also got a new bus station between Market Street and Ganny Road, roads which for practical purpose all but ceased to exist. By 2008 major plans for an even newer improved bus station were in hand.

WORKING LIFE

Below: Hartley's Sewing Shop in Hebden Bridge was just one of many that had recently opened for business in 1910 as the growth in the ready to wear clothing industry took hold. Although the women worked hard, it was far less dangerous employment than working in the textile mills where large scale machinery could crush someone or lop off a few fingers quite easily. There was also less chance of a fire breaking out as the raw material which this workforce used was already woven into cloth. Although in use in the early 19th century, it was Isaac Singer whose name became synonymous with the sewing machine. In the 1850s, he adapted the ideas of others to produce his own model and had a double brainwave. Firstly, he formed a hire purchase company so that people could afford his machines and buy them 'on the drip'. Then, he went into mass production of smaller models that could be used at home, rather than the larger ones intended for tailoring. An empire was born and the Singer company went on to be the first to introduce electric machines in 1889.

Top right: Work in the winding room at Joshua Smith's Frostholme Mill, at Cornholme, came to a brief halt for the photographer to capture this image. At one time this large cotton mill employed more than 700 people, making it one of the area's major employers. The firm of Joshua Smith operated the mill for over 70 years, from the early 1880s until the 1950s. The photograph was taken in 1913, just a year before the outbreak of the First World War. Clearly the winding of cotton yard onto bobbins was regarded as 'women's work'. In stark contrast with the women in their aprons standing by their machinery is someone apparently rather more senior in the mill – a man wearing suit, collar and tie. Women knew their place in those days! Compared to other forms of employment, however, mill work was relatively well paid, and would shortly become even more so. Domestic service, becoming a maid or cook, was one of the most common occupations for women at the time. The outbreak of war in 1914 leading to millions of men joining the forces created a huge labour shortage in industry. Women took over many of the jobs previously done by men. Wages rose and big houses were soon denuded of servants who discovered that mill work not only paid infinitely better than the pittance commonly paid to servants, but also gave them the freedom to do what they liked in their own time, a luxury often not granted in domestic service.

Below right: Waistcoats, flat cap and 'short back and sides' date this workplace scene more readily than any label. More than half a century ago any respectable chap wore a collar and tie at work no matter how humble his station in life. Not that pattern cutting could be considered particularly low on the scale of things. Cutting out pieces of cloth to be made into jackets, trousers —and of course those waistcoats - required no little skill if expensive cloth was not to be wasted and profits eaten away. The skill lay not just in ensuring the most economic use of cloth but also in making sure than any pattern in the cloth would match when sewn together. Corduroy and fustian were the materials to found in this Hebden Bridge factory and were renowned for their hardwearing qualities. The concept of a 'throwaway' society was unimaginable in these far off days: men who bought clothes expected them to last, if not for a lifetime, then at least for decades. A man's 'Sunday Best' might be worn only for Church on Sunday, to be married in and finally in his coffin. Though

working clothes may have been bought 'ready-made' the same could not be said for 'Sunday' best'. A man's best suit would invariably still made to measure by a tailor. Not until the late 1960s would the sale of off the peg men's suits overtake those which had been made to individual specifications. The cost difference however was not always as great as might be expected.

Above: The tram route to West Vale was opened on 29 May, 1914. The construction of the Victoria Road section attracted a number of onlookers who enjoyed watching other people sweating as they swung their picks into the unforgiving ground. Householders peered out of their windows or from their front doorsteps. Although they could appreciate the benefits that the new tramline would bring, most were not too keen on having the noise and disruption that went with it. When completed, the racket of the tramcars rumbling past would give them something else to moan about. This was an early example of what would be known as Nimby (not in my back yard) later in the century.

When completed, the trams at West Vale could link with the lines into Halifax, as well as with Elland, Birchencliffe, Edgerton and Huddersfield. Victoria Road itself connects Elland town centre with Hammerstones Lane that leads away towards Holywell Green.

Bottom left: The rather odd looking device was the machine used to insert cat's eyes, or reflecting roadstud units as they were grandly named, into the highway. The units consisted of two pairs of reflective glass spheres set into a rubber dome and mounted into a cast iron housing. Probably used here on Wakefield Road, the glass and rubber domes generally had one pair of cat's eye showing in each direction. A fixed rubber wiper cleans the surface as they sink below the surface. In 1934 Percy Shaw patented his invention, that put Boothtown on the industrial map, and they were a special boon during the blackout in World War II. This gave a huge boost to production and the firm grew in size making more than a million roadstuds a year, which were exported worldwide. The use of shuttered headlights on cars during that period made Shaw's invention particularly important. The government encouraged production so that almost all of the country's major roads were fitted with cat's eyes by the time that peace was declared. After the war, a Ministry of Transport committee led by James Callaghan encouraged further production so that as many of our roads as possible could be included. There are several versions of how Percy Shaw was inspired to come up with his invention, from seeing a real cat looking back at him from the side of the road to seeing reflections from tramlines, but whatever the truth, motorists are grateful to him.

Above right: Pictured in 1956, these women are not involved in some sort of manufacture of glass eyes for those who require a socket plugging. They were involved in the assembly of one of the most influential, yet simplest, road safety measures ever dreamed up. This workforce was part of Percy Shaw's Reflecting Roadstud company that manufactured cat's eyes and earned the Halifax man a fortune and a place in the history books as an inventor of renown. Shaw was born in Halifax, the son of James Shaw a dyehouse labourer. He had humble beginnings, leaving school at 13 and working at a blanket mill carrying bobbins of wool from the winders to the weavers, but went on to become a household name. The factory in Boothtown was situated not far from the place that was his home for all but two of his eighty-six years. Despite his comfortable financial position, Percy lived a generally Spartan life, though he did enjoy a couple of luxuries, namely his two Rolls Royce cars. Such was the success of his invention that he was awarded the OBE in 1965 for his services to exports. His business is still going strong on Mill Lane, Boothtown, more than 30 years after he left us.

Below: A woman's work is never done. Never has that been more the case than when applied to a rural setting. Out in the countryside, there was no easy life for women who relied on the good soil of England to provide them with a living. They tilled the land with hand tools, fetched in the crops and milked the cows without the help of electrical aids and petrol driven machinery. When day was done, it was back home to face a round of cooking, cleaning and nurturing. At the end of the 19th century life expectancy was just 45 years. The traditional three score years and ten was for those who had a life of privilege. The work that these country girls carried out laid down the foundation for more formal organisations that were required in the world wars that were to come in the 20th century. When the menfolk marched off to fight in 1914 and again in 1939, there was a huge void left behind. In 1915 the Board of Agriculture actively encouraged women to become farm labourers, though traditional male farmers had to be persuaded to accept them. By 1917 some quarter of a million girls and women were working the land. The Women's Land Army was even more formally organised in the Second World War when conscription was introduced.

Top right: Were it not for the dress of the onlookers and the tram tracks in the road this might be a modern picture of a vintage vehicle rally rather than the 1930s. The scene is Todmorden in the upper Calder Valley, but what occasion merits such an impressive turnout including not only Todmorden's Fire Brigade, but also a fine Rolls Royce car is unrecorded. The fire engine at the head of the parade was already a little long in the tooth. On Saturday 3rd October 1914 local dignitaries and visitors from nearby towns met at Todmorden Fire Station to witness the arrival of the new motor fire engine. Freshly painted in vermilion-coloured livery, the new engine was fitted with a 4-cylinder petrol-driven motor capable of delivering 60-70 horse power and of speeds of up to 40mph. The new engine was delivered by its makers, Merryweather & Co. of London. In the early afternoon the visitors and officials boarded a specially chartered bus to follow the new fire engine to Hare Mill (subsequently known as Mons Mill). Once at the mill the engine's powerful 'Hatfield' pump was put through its paces. In the first trial, using two 75 ft lengths of hose and a pressure of 180 lbs, the water jet was seen to reach a point just short of the word 'Hare' on the mill's chimney, claimed to be over a hundred feet above the ground. Housed at what is now 'the old Fire Station', Todmorden Fire Service moved into new premises in 1969.

Below right: This street scene captured in the early 1960s depicts workmen at the bottom of Bramston Street at Bridge End, where Brighouse gives way to Rastrick. The contractors working on behalf of the Borough Council are laying a new pipeline which was to pass through Brighouse town centre and on to Wakefield Road. On the left of the photograph the building covered in advertising hoardings is today the successful Bridge End nursery school. Most of the property on the right of the scene has been demolished. For small boys in particular such a scene was an absolute magnet. Watching the heavy plant in use was utterly fascinating. In the foreground is a quite modern looking road roller, the diesel powered replacement for a real 'steam roller' though, even today still often called a steam roller though it is half a century or more since the genuine article was ever used. Behind the road roller is a far more venerable machine, one which today looks decidedly ancient. Superficially similar looking diesel-powered cranes and diggers were to be found in many settings from quarrying to road building. They had evolved from steam-powered ancestors, and their caterpillar tracks had appeared first on agricultural steam engines before being applied to tanks in the first world war. By the end of the 1960s such machinery which used winches to raise and lower the shovel were history as hydraulic arms replaced wire ropes and bright yellow steel cabs superseded wooden 'sheds'.

What a busy scene are these pictures showing Halifax Piece Hall during its ignominious time as a wholesale market. The predominance of horses and carts over motor vehicles firmly dates the scene to the period not long after the First World War. One of Halifax's 'Crown Jewels' the Piece Hall opened on 1 January, 1779, as a place for local merchants to sell pieces of cloth produced by handloom weavers. With the industrial revolution, however, handloom weaving disappeared and with it the Piece Hall's purpose. In 1868 ownership of the Piece Hall passed to Halifax Corporation, which in 1871 moved the wholesale fish, game, fruit and vegetable market there. To improve access the south gateway was enlarged, whilst for improved security ornate iron gates were installed. A moveable footbridge was built over the gateway allowing larger vehicles to enter. The upper-floors were all but abandoned, whilst more easily accessible lean-to buildings and sheds began to clutter the once wide-open courtyard. By the time these photographs were taken the Piece Hall was about to become a scheduled monument, but its future remained in doubt. Many proposals were put forward, from converting it into a swimming pool to providing cheap accommodation for the unemployed. Hidden behind other buildings, and rarely visited by the public, by the 1970s the Piece Hall was forgotten by many. In 1972 however the Department of the Environment gave the Piece Hall Grade One listing making it impossible to demolish. Before long the market was moved elsewhere, and the Piece Hall restored to its former glory.

Here is an awesome scene of activity as one of the largest feats of civil engineering ever undertaken in Halifax takes shape. A new by-pass road from King Cross to Godley cutting, avoiding the town centre, had been planned in 1964. John Burdock, a prominent alderman and highways committee chairman, had been the moving force behind the scheme for a bypass to ease the congestion. Pride of place in the new road scheme would be a new bridge across the Hebble, far above the existing North Bridge. The cast iron parapet and roadbed of North Bridge can just be glimpsed on the far left almost hidden by scaffolding. The new flyover would be at least the fourth bridge to span the Hebble at this point. An earlier great stone bridge was demolished when North Bridge was built in the 19th century.However, a far earlier and much smaller bridge still exists. Old Lane which can be seem at the bottom of the photograph, crosses the Hebble below these gigantic works. Construction began in 1970. The road finally opened to traffic in 1973. Around 60,000 residents of Halifax took the opportunity to explore the new bypass close up - a 'walkabout' was held on the unopened road. At the opening ceremony, conducted by Halifax Mayor Ald. Maurice Jagger, the road was officially named Burdock Way after the man who had done so much to promote it.

Freudenberg Nonwovens LP

Today it is locally based in the Lowfields Business Park, Elland, but Freudenberg Nonwovens LP is not only an international company but also one which has its origins in quite another place and another time.

It was in 1849 that Carl Johann Freudenberg and his partner Heinrich Christian Heintze took over a tannery in the Müllheim valley near Weinheim southern Germany after the liquidation of the Heintze and Sammet company. There the partners set up a high quality leather business which not only prospered but also achieved important trade links worldwide.

With new, fashionable products, such as patent leather and satin leather, the company grew and exported all over the world throughout the Victorian era.

Between 1900 and 1904, in the course of his own experiments, Hermann Ernst Freudenberg, son of the

company's founder, became the first manufacturer in Europe to develop a tanning process using chrome liquor instead of vegetable dyes. This invention reduced production time by months, and Freudenberg became one of the biggest tanneries in Europe.

The four years of the First World War, subsequent currency inflation, and the economic crisis of 1929, hit the company hard. Until then, 60-70% of the leather produced had been exported. Exports suddenly became impossible, and the founder's grandchildren faced the question: Where do we go from here?

Above: *A 1960s view of the delivery end of the batching machine.* ***Below:*** *By simply looking at the fashions shown one can date this picture to the 1960s. This was Bondina's Vilene Studio, the workshop of clothing technicians who 'served industry and the public'. It was the 'testing ground' for applications and performance of existing products and new developments.*

The grandchildren of company founder Carl Johann Freudenberg - engineer Hans Freudenberg, personnel and finance manager Richard Freudenberg, sales manager Otto Freudenberg and purchasing manager Walter Freudenberg - ventured out on a new enterprise strategy.

First, they began by reworking leather residues and then developing substitute materials for leather. For example, from 1929, the company started manufacturing leather seals and from 1936 radial shaft seals with a sealing lip made of 'Perbunan' synthetic rubber. The trade name for these radial shaft seals - 'Simmerring' - became a technical term in its own right.

The company still deals with the automotive industry and in 1956 it developed metal-to-rubber bonded components that control vibrations in engines and transmission units.

In 1948, however, the company's experiments in leather processing led to the development of a new type of material, 'nonwovens'. This was a very versatile, sheet like structure with textile characteristics. Freudenberg is still the world's premier producers of nonwovens.

The post-war reconstruction period also brought the opportunity to invest again outside Germany. Before the war the company had operated production sites in Austria, Switzerland, France and Great Britain.

Meanwhile, in Greetland, near Halifax, there was a mill popularly known as Belle Isle owned by The Bradford Dyers' Association Ltd, a combination of Bradford dyeing firms, founded in 1898. Shortly after the turn of the 20th century, workers had begun appearing there in clogs, corduroys and red mufflers and smoking clay pipes. The office workers would stand at high desks and only the typists were allowed to sit. The dye workers were given just a twenty minute break for their lunch, and even the managers had to 'clock on' alongside the workers. There were no holidays with pay, the dyehouse was freezing and the work was heavy; but in spite of this, according to the memories of Mr. Harry Parr, an employee for 50 years, the workers were usually in good spirits. Work was scarce sometimes, but it was shared out equally so that no-one was sacked.

Mr Parr would recall many 'characters' from the early days. Jack Sharp, a manager, cooked his own dinner in his office every day. Walt Smith, a shop floor worker, was a knur and spell player and keen clay pigeon shooter. A fitter, Fred Barker, carried two steel rules, one for work and one to

stir his tea! Once a week, 'Tripe Joe' Kitson would bring a large basket to work to sell his tripe to the workers. At certain times during the day, the works buzzer sounded and local people set their clocks by it. The dye works had an efficient fire brigade that held weekly practices.

In 1923/4, Bradford Dyers' Association built two blocks of houses, known as Silverdale Terrace, for its own people to

*Top left: Cross laying the carding fleece. **Left:** The blended fibre, ready for the next stage in the production process - 'carding'. **Above:** A section of the laboratory where all Bondina products were subjected to the most exacting tests to guarantee the reliability of standards.*

buy. After a £45 government subsidy the sale price to workers was £445 each, which they paid at a few shillings a week.

The canteen was three ex-army huts. For a charge of one penny, the canteen staff would cook whatever food the workers brought with them for lunch.

In 1925/6 a Silk department opened, but in 1929 the dyeing and finishing of woollen cloth stopped. Some of the woollen workers transferred to the silkworks but many were left out of work.

Early in 1950 an Irishman, Bill Blackwood, set up an importing business. He operated from London, making arrangements with the Viledon department in Weinheim to market Freudenberg's products within the UK.

He created the name Vilene and registered his company as Vilene Ltd. Blackwood's business however, ran into difficulties in 1954, partly because of the cheap fibres available already in Britain and partly because of import tariffs.

Bill Blackwood decided it would be a good idea if the goods were manufactured in England. He was acquainted with a director of the Bradford Dyers' Association, Eric Padgett, and BDA had done Dyeing and finishing for Freudenberg in the past. BDA had space available and, eventually,

Freudenberg's chose the Greetland site to begin operations in this country. In 1956 the first lot of machinery was shipped over and installed in the 80,000 square feet of space. Work was under way by May 1956 and the first sales made in September.

The new company was named BONDINA. It had an initial staff of 15, most of whom continuing working for the business until their retirement. Premises were also leased in London, in St. James Street, where Bondina Sales Ltd. was formed.

'Vilene', Bondina's trade name for its nonwoven interlining product, became a well-known brand name. At its peak production the complex would occupy more than a quarter of a million square feet.

Meanwhile BDA was having further setbacks. Nylon had become an increasingly popular material for lingerie, and as it could not process nylon, the company at Greetland closed and Freudenberg took over all the space. It was a

Top: At the time of this picture dating from 1969, this was the largest finished stock warehouse in the country and was capable of holding 3 million yards of Vilene. The sheer size can be discerned by the tiny figure of a woman (bottom centre). **Left:** *The Stenter Finishing Range.*

very amicable arrangement. BDA's partners expressed appreciation of all past contacts with Freudenberg, and, on the latter's behalf, Professor Kraft said they had had "not only a partnership but a friendship."

But BDA had steadily declined, and by 1962 all its operations moved from the Greetland location. So, within six years, Bondina had taken over the whole site. In 1964 the BDA was taken over by the Viyella Group.

Meanwhile, as the demand for nonwovens increased, several extensions were added to the original buildings. 1968 saw the first of these, and the second in 1974, whilst the two phases of the fourth building came in 1988/9. By then the total floor space was 50,000 square feet and Bondina was one of the foremost producers of nonwovens in the UK.

But what were these 'nonwovens'?

Carefully selected mixtures of natural and man made fibres were blended in varying combinations according to the properties required in the finished fabric. The fibres were fed direct to the production line. A uniform fibre fleece was achieved by a special carding technique. The web produced was impregnated with synthetic latex foam and fed into a curing oven. When the web was thoroughly bonded, it was thoroughly washed, and finishing processes were applied to achieve the qualities demanded, washability, hard or soft handling, etc.

The company was proud to be awarded the British Standards Institution BS 5750 (Part 2). The demand grew for Vilene Interlining, the best-known product of its kind in both the clothing industry and in home dressmaking. About this time, the Vilene Studio was formed to offer a unique technical advisory service. In the studio, clothing technicians checked all applications of Vilene before recommending it to a manufacturer. They were constantly at the disposal of the clothing industry.

Applications for the product were found outside the clothing industry. It was suitable for insulation materials in the electrical industry, filters for heating and ventilating, backing for PVC coating industry, and interlining for shoes. It was used for the sound insulation of aircraft, for battery separators, the manufacture of handbags and luggage and cleaning cloths. The company developed nylon-based abrasive materials for household, industrial and catering use. It

Top: *The open plan sales administration office. It is difficult to imagine that in those days computers were practically unheard of. No self-respecting office today would be without one, yet back then, the work still got done and all of it done manually!*

Left: *The staff canteen at the Greetland factory, circa 1965. This picture is included because it has a famous face on it! Sitting at the table in the foreground, facing the camera is Gordon Kaye, star of the TV situation comedy 'Allo allo,' who worked for Bondina in the 1960s.*

medical and pharmaceutical sector, is continually gaining ground. A small share of products are sold to final users under the Vileda, O'Cedar and Wettex brands

Freudenberg remains a family company. It is owned by some 300 heirs to the founding father Carl Johann Freudenberg.

In addition to its Elland site Freudenberg Nonwovens comprises 22 other production facilities in 13 different countries, employs over 4,800 people and generates annual revenues of over $1 Billion. Freudenberg Nonwovens was not only one of the first to introduce nonwovens to the market, but is the largest and most diverse manufacturer of nonwovens in the world.

Recent developments include Evolon, a new innovative process for the production of nonwovens which was developed in Weinheim at the beginning of the new millennium: water jet stabilized micro-fibre nonwovens are produced in a single continuous process from polymer granulates to textile sheet. Thanks to this technology, nonwovens can also be used as a material for clothing, decoration and tableware.

contributed to the production of protective suits for the armed forces for use at home and abroad against chemical and biological warfare, and civilian protection against poisonous gases.

Currently 'Mechatronics' – new 'intelligent 3D' integration and crimping technologies are under development, whilst innovative products such as fuel cell seals, gas diffusion layers and filters based on nonwovens are under development.

In 1970 the holding company moved into electronics technology with computer accessories and printed circuit boards added to their product range.

Today, in the 21st century, Carl Johann Freudenberg's legacy of innovation and investment shows no sign of flagging.

In 2000 Vilene developed 'Smart Textile' products which generated great interest from customers and allowed for greater diversity.

Today the Freudenberg Group comprises 13 Business Groups operating independently on various markets all over the world. As a family company it is guided by long-term orientation, financial solidity and the excellence of our people in 53 countries around the globe.

Top left: 1990s view of the old Greetland factory.
Left and below: Freudenberg's Lowfields Business Park, Elland premises.

The Group supplies seals, vibration control technology components, filters, nonwovens, release agents and lubricants to almost all of the world's vehicle manufacturers, and the significance of customers from other branches of industry, such as mechanical and plant engineering, the energy and chemical industry or the

Fan Systems Group

It is a testament to the diversity of the applications of technology, that the Fan Systems Group has spent more than half a century exploring and developing, that many readers will have bought or consumed a product aided by the company's Manufacture.

Fan Systems Group Ltd is the leading UK manufacturer of bespoke industrial fans and part of the global Witt Group of companies.

Above and below: Fans ready for despatch in the early 1950s. Right: Fan destined for a former Halifax brickworks.

The company manufactures its centrifugal and axial fans from two factories situated at Holywell Green and Greetland, just outside Halifax. In its early days Fan Systems started to supply the UK Nuclear Industry, and it continues to do so today, as one of the few accredited fan suppliers to that Industry.

Fan Systems Ltd was established on 16 March, 1950, by three employees of another fan company, Musgrave Fans. These three, Messrs Murphy, Simkins and Vaudrey, based the company in Piccadilly, Manchester, and expanded the business rapidly, supplying industrial fans and drying systems to their numerous customers.

Mr Murphy was the Managing Director, Mr Vaudrey was involved with the supply of equipment to the glass industry and Mr Simkins took responsibility for supplying fans to the heavy clay industry.

Fan Systems has remained one of the foremost suppliers of fans to the Nuclear Industry. It took the first orders from the then Atomic Energy Board in 1950. Since then the company has been continually and actively involved in the design of systems, working in partnership with nuclear construction engineers to achieve the optimum solutions to meet the stringent demands of the industry.

With increasing success however, the Piccadilly site became inadequate, and in 1954 it became necessary to relocate to another Manchester site.

Initially a large proportion of production was subcontracted to other engineering companies but from 1957 the company started fan production in Slaithwaite, near Huddersfield.

Fan Systems took over the manufacture of fans from a company called Andrew Weatherfoils in 1963, and in doing so acquired drawings of new fan designs as well as a number of high profile customers involved in the nuclear industry; clients who have remained with the company ever since. Other sectors supplied with numerous centrifugal fans were the heavy-clay, ceramic,

Top: A consignment of fans leaving for a Scottish microchip manufacturer. Left: Direct driven centrifugal fan for a soap manufacturer in Lancashire. Below: Manufacture of fans.

Expanding further in 1965, Fan Systems took over PM Walker, which produced its own fans as well as being involved in air conditioning and sheet metal working.

Turnover steadied from the late 1970s onwards, and sales strategy became more aggressive. The company started to supply new industries including the paper drying and automotive industry, their clients included such big names as Hyundai and Ford.

Top left: V Belt Driven fans for the tobacco industry (1980s). *Above:* An oxidiser plant in Derbyshire where the firm's fans are installed (1990s). *Below:* Two size 48 NA Type Fans with Energy Storing Flywheel Drives (1970s), for use with a Thermal Chemical Plant Oxidiser Installation in Scotland.

tobacco and carpet industries, not least the famous Dean Clough operation in Halifax.

Systems and acquired the company.

Based near Hamburg, Witt & Sohn had been established in the late 1940s as a specialised manufacturer of fans to the German merchant shipbuilding industry. Its well-proven expertise in axial and centrifugal fan manufacture has made it market leader in many specialised high performance sectors. It is no idle boast that Witt fans are used on in excess of 12,000 ships globally - this figure represents approximately 10 per cent of the current world-wide fleet. Witt brought an unparalleled level of technology to the Halifax-based company, and henceforth Fan Systems had access to a wider range

In 1978 the company moved offices and production to its site in Greetland, Halifax. Remarkably the physical framework of the factory was built from what had been the former Blackpool Railway Station. The Managing Director of PM Walker at the time had spotted the station being dismantled and put in an offer for the structure - the building is still in use today.

Production and turnover steadied in the 1980s as the company concentrated on the sale of specialised centrifugal fans to a number of core businesses. This action enabled the company to survive the recession of the early 1990s, but it was not expanding as quickly as the Directors would have liked.

In 1993, Fan Systems was acquired by the Witt Group, a German based manufacturer of fans, which has production facilities throughout the world. In addition, it has licenses to manufacture in countries such as Japan, Korea, Canada and Indonesia.

The solution came in 1993 when the Witt Group, a German based manufacturer of fans, which has production facilities throughout the world and has licenses to manufacture in countries such as Japan, Korea, Canada and Indonesia, recognised the untapped potential in Fan

Top left: Fan Systems are heavily involved in the Nuclear Industry. *Left:* The launch of Wave Knight, with centrifugal fans provided by Fan Systems, 2000. *Below:* One of a pair of Fan Silencers for Canterbury Hospital, 2000.

of fans which it had previously been unable to supply. The companies' range of fans complemented each other well, and by 1999 turnover had grown to a figure in excess of £3 million.

Fan Systems has benefited greatly from its takeover by the Witt Group which allowed it to enter new, highly specialised markets. Its products are now used by some of the world's most famous companies, including Rolls Royce, Shell, Astra Zeneca, Alstom, Daimler Benz, BNFL as well as being installed on a large number of naval vessels.

The extensive Witt range of fans and its design programme were integrated into Fan Systems' expanded CAD facilities. This now enabled Fan Systems to give a rapid turnaround, typically within 48 hours, for quotations and all support documentation. It also was now able to offer fan specifications on disk to enable customers to make their own fan selection and noise calculations.

Underlining both Fan Systems' and Witt's philosophy is a commitment to total quality, Witt procedures have

been certified to comply with the German nuclear and marine quality standards, and it was one of the first companies to achieve accreditation to ISO 9001 TÜV.

There are presently 40 on-site staff locally, and a well established Service and Maintenance Division. Every fan manufactured is test run and quality recorded to ensure optimum customer satisfaction with the quality and performance of the fans produced and supplied. Fan Systems is a progressive company and believes in continually striving to improve the products it offers. The research and development budget is on average five per cent of the annual company turnover.

Fan Systems firmly believe that its commitment to the

Above: Alister Bush, Factory Manager at the Greetland site, with one of two fans being inspected prior to plastic coating.
Below left: Impulse Fans for underground car parks.
Below: 8 off Axle Fans 1,120mm diameter.

and Management departments Martin Downs has spent more than 40 years in the fan industry.

Today, more than half a century since it began, the Fan Systems Group more than lives up to its founder's hopes and aspirations.

Top: Two Galvanised Air Pollution Fans for a Sewage Plant ready for transportation on a Collett heavy goods transport vehicle. **Left:** *Twenty fans ready for assembly prior to shipment to Denmark.* **Below:** *Martin Booth, Managing Director of UK operation.*

customer does not end with the supply of the fan to site. Records have been kept for every fan manufactured in over sixty years of the company's history. A network of engineers across the country has been established to offer advice and provide after sales service to ensure that all customer expectations are met.

The firm has always been an excellent employer, providing employees with a good working environment, and in return many of its staff have remained with the company for decades. Tony Mitchell and David Sykes have worked in the factory for over 35 years. In the Sales

Thornbers - Well Hatched Plans

From a dozen hens kept in orange boxes in a backyard, to the biggest company of its kind in the world – that's the amazing story of Thornbers, the Mytholmroyd-based business that transformed the Upper Calder Valley.

Though its chickens are now history Thornbers remains one the area's most important and influential business names.

This is the remarkable tale of an enterprise that started in a very small way but which developed into a world leader, at its peak employing nearly 1,500 people.

The Thornbers story begins when Edgar Thornber was born at Laneside in Mytholmroyd, Hebden Bridge in 1888. He was the second son of Lettice and Robert Thornber, who in the 1891 census is recorded as being a fustian dyer. Because his parents were ordinary working folk Edgar began work at the age of 11, as a half-timer, going to school for half the day and working in a local mill for the other half.

Edgar was 13 when he began full-time work.

By 1906 the family had moved to Mayroyd in Hebden Bridge. That year an event took place which was to change Edgar's life – the fustian weavers of Hebden Bridge went on strike. The weavers were dissatisfied with the fact that their wages were lower than those paid in Lancashire. The Hebden Bridge mill owners claimed that their transport costs were much higher – raw cotton which came into the country via Liverpool and Manchester having to be brought much further. The strike was to last for nearly two and a half years. Meanwhile Edgar, young and energetic, was not going to sit around waiting for its end – he had ideas.

Keeping poultry for showing was a popular hobby at the time, and generated great rivalry. Birds were bred and selected for their exhibition points. Farmers' wives would have a few hens scratching around outside producing eggs during the summer, and these may well have been birds that were not considered good enough for showing. At that time no one really thought about selecting birds for their egg-laying capabilities, and the housing of poultry was rather primitive.

With time on his hands Edgar decided to turn a hobby into a business and set up a hatchery. He acquired a few orange boxes, some broody hens and some eggs and set these up in the back yard at Mayroyd, protected only by bits of sacking.

*Top left: Founder Edgar Thornber. **Bottom left:** Mayroyd Hebden Bridge, circa 1906. **Below:** Newhouse Farm, purchased by Edgar Thornber in 1913. **Above:** An early Gloucester Incubator.*

The first sittings must have been a success, as we know that with his brother Ralph's help at evenings and weekends, Edgar quickly increased the number of broody hens from around a dozen to 300.

Once this enterprise was launched Edgar was never to go back to work in the mill again.

Edgar spent considerable time scouring the countryside to find hens and the fertilised eggs for them to sit upon. 'Hatching' eggs were about three shillings and sixpence (17 1/2p) a dozen, and there were times when he was hard pressed to find the money to buy them. Edgar's mother dipped into her modest purse to help, but it was the proud boast of the Thornbers that a total of no more than £25 was originally invested in the enterprise: rather, everything that was made, apart from modest living expenses, was put back into the business.

With such rapid expansion and success Edgar soon exhausted the local market. Very early he was placing adverts in Poultry World and other magazines. He was also travelling as far afield as Shudehill Market in Manchester to sell his chicks.

Even in those early days parent stock was carefully selected, and birds with any suggestion of weakness were ruthlessly rejected. That was how the Thornber reputation for quality was established.

Artificial incubation was then only just coming into use. The majority of people looked at incubators with suspicion, but technology was an area that Edgar was never afraid to investigate. His first egg incubator, a 'Hearson', was housed in Edgar's bedroom.

The cottage at Mayroyd however, was rented, and the blossoming poultry business was not appreciated by the landlord who lived in the big house next door.

Inevitably the Thornber family was invited to find other accommodation.

In 1911 the family moved as tenants to Newhouse Farm. Now the orange boxes could be discarded as the 23-year old Edgar converted the barn into an incubator room.

Top: Loading chicks on the farm ready for transportation. ***Centre:*** *Ben Stansfield designer of the 'Silver Hen' chick rearer.* **Left:** *Square Works, Mytholmroyd.*

The four acres of land at the farm were put to good use with breeding pens.

Soon Edgar had progressed to 12 'Gloucester' incubators, each of which had a capacity of 390 eggs. Initially these were oil-heated, though they were later changed to gas. The majority of business was conducted by mail order, cash with order - so Edgar was effectively able to build up his business using his customers' money.

Arrangements were made with the Lancashire and Yorkshire Railway Company for newly-hatched chicks to be transported by fast passenger train.

Though tiny, apparently fragile things, a day-old chick can easily stand such treatment. The chick actually develops from the white of the egg around the yolk which provides a source of nourishment for up to 48 hours after it has hatched.

Initially purebred stock was the main business; and Edgar was hatching eggs from 20-30 varieties of poultry. Gradually however, crossbred pullets for egg laying were introduced. Geese and turkeys too came on the scene.

The business had been built up exclusively on livestock, but soon after the family moved to Newhouse Farm a friendship developed between Edgar and Ben Stansfield which would lead to important changes.

Ben Stansfield was a partner in a sheet metal business in Hebden Bridge. It was Ben who designed 'Silver Hen' chick rearers and other equipment which would be sold by 'Thornber Bros'. As a

Top: Devastation caused by the 'flash back' at Kynock plant in 1928. *Left:* The Elphaborough Estate purchased in 1928. *Above:* Newhouse Farm was one of Thornbers Experimental Poultry Breeding Farms.

result, in 1913, the appliance side of the business began. That same year another major step was taken: Thornbers bought Newhouse Farm.

Any optimism in 1913 was soon dissipated the next year which saw the start of the First World War. During the war years of 1914-18 the firm may have bravely used the slogan 'Business As Usual', but times were actually far from usual. Ralph Thornber went off into the Royal Flying Corps – forerunner of the RAF. At home Edgar carried on alone, doing his bit in the Local Defence Corps at evenings and weekends. Ben Stansfield used any time he could spare to keep an eye on the administrative side of things.

Poultry keepers found that their supplies of grain were severely restricted, although this was later helped by supplies of 'ship-wrecked grain' classified as unfit for human consumption. The price of hatching eggs rose to between six and seven shillings a dozen (30-40p), twice the price they had been before the war. But there remained a good demand for chicks. Other prices included purebred pullets, available from January to April each year at 12s 6d (62 1/2p), whilst 'exhibition' specimens ranged in price from that same price up to an astonishing £20.

During the war the appliance side of the business was cut back. By the early 1920s however, such was the demand that a mill known as Square Works was taken over by Thornbers. The sawdust produced in cutting timber at the mill was used in a 'Kynock' gas production plant to provide power, thus the waste from one section drove the two engines which powered the works.

In 1928 however, there was a flashback from the gas plant. Burning shavings scattered over the mill causing a disastrous fire. Attending fire engines

Top left: Cyril Thornber, former Chairman and Managing Director joined the company in 1937. **Top right and above:** By the 1960s rail delivery was replaced by road transportation. Above are two of Thornbers A40 Austin delivery vans from the 1950s and 1960s. **Below:** Staff pictured at a company conference in Blackpool in 1959.

pumped water for a whole week. In total the fire cost Thornbers some £10,000.

Such a terrible setback was not to deter further progress. In the early 1930s Edgar, together with a Lancashire duck breeder developed a new duck, based on the Aylesbury, which would fatten quickly and hatch all year round. At the Elphaborough Estate, which had been purchased in 1928, Thornbers were soon raising a million ducks a year.

In 1937, by which time Thornbers output was 3,500,000 chicks and ducks, Cyril Thornber joined the staff. Straight from school he passed from one department to another learning the job the hard way.

With the start of the Second World War two years later Thornbers business was not as badly affected as many others. Grain rationing was based on the numbers of stock at the outbreak of war and Thornbers stocks were very high at the time a census was taken. Even so ducks were considered a luxury and that side of the business was much reduced.

Meanwhile householders were encouraged to raise hens of their own. This created a large demand for chicks from Thornbers.

Edgar Thornber died in 1944. Though having built up a business with an annual turnover of £200,000 he had little interest in wealth for its own sake, taking more pleasure from his garden than in money.

Now at the age of just 23 Cyril Thornber found himself with the responsibility of running a large firm – at the centre of one of the greatest concentrations of hatcheries in the world. Thanks to

Thornbers and others, Mytholmroyd railway station was despatching up to 2,000 consignments of day old chicks per day.

During the 1950s Thornbers introduced battery cages as the most economic method of rearing chickens and sold them around the world.

Meanwhile in the late 1940s Cyril had been to the USA and met Henry Wallace who later visited Mytholmroyd. Wallace was an expert in breeding hybrid chickens, combining the best characteristics to produce the perfect bird. The result was the 404, which laid brown eggs, and would be the most popular chicken ever bred in Britain. By 1974 Thornbers had sold 250 million. The breeding programme which led to the 404 was helped by the introduction of a computer in 1962. The Elliott 803 cost £30,000 and was one of the first such devices in Britain. It was used for genetic research, accountancy and data processing.

Top left: *Cyril pictured with Prince Philip at Olympia Poultry Show in the 1960s.* **Above and left:** *Celebrating the 200th Million 404 chick (pictured left).* **Below:** *In testing over 300,000 birds each year in the 1960s, some 25 million calculations were needed. The Elliot 803 computer was a small cog in the wheel that made these results possible.*

Yet all was not well. Foreign competition began to eat away at the viability of British producers, and by the late 1960s the writing was on the wall for Thornbers. In 1972 the business was sold to Pentos holdings. However, Cyril Thornber managed to keep two poultry farms and his breeding stock. Cyril and his wife Dorothy moved from the family home Rose Mount to a bungalow, creating a spectacular garden there.

In 1991 Cyril passed away quietly in his armchair having spent a busy day negotiating with Ministry of Agriculture officials. Following Cyril's death the family decided to discontinue with poultry altogether. A difficult decision after 84 years, but a necessary one. During the last twenty years Cyril's son, Ralph Thornber, having recognised the need locally for business premises to rent, has been instrumental in turning the company's under-used properties into units to let.

The company bought back the Hoo Hole Works, its former poultry equipment factory, and then Square Works in Mytholmroyd, its former office and joinery division. This was renamed Orchard Business Park. Once those and other properties were occupied, Ralph turned his attention to the two poultry farms at Dean Hey and Top Land. Today there is an impressive entrance to Dean Hey and Top Land Country Business Parks on Cragg Road Mytholmroyd. They provide an ideal working environment with modern facilities in a peaceful and picturesque setting but with access to all amenities, lots of parking and 24-hour security.

The 'Ark' Day Nursery, the brain-child of Ralph's daughter, is one of the most successful in the North. It sits happily alongside several other businesses, housed in state of the art offices in the former

poultry buildings at Dean Hey. Just along the road Top Land Country Business Park is home to some 18 businesses varying from a manufacturer of prayer mats to a gym.

Today Ralph Thornber is responsible for day-to-day management of Thornber properties. He takes great pride in the fact that the company is one of the major providers of commercial property for rent in the Upper Calder Valley, supplying premises for businesses employing over a 1,000 people.

Thornbers is still a family business. Ralph and his sisters are Directors of the Company. Their mother, Dorothy, still keeps an eye on what's happening from the bungalow at Dean Hey.

Cyril Thornber would be proud to see how his and his father's legacy has flourished. With the fourth generation of the family now starting to become involved, and a fifth generation growing up in and around Mytholmroyd, the Thornber name looks set to remain one to remember for many years yet to come.

Top left: *The advertising of Thornbers Orchard Business Park industrial units and offices.* *Top right:* *A view overlooking Top Land Country Business Park.* *Above:* *The entrance drive to Top Land and Dean Hey Country Business Parks.* *Below:* *A bird's eye view of Dean Hey Country Business Park, Cragg Road, Mytholmroyd.*

HBOS - Halifax at its Best

Travel to any part of Britain and say you are from Halifax, and the response is invariably the same - 'Ah, the Building Society!' The Halifax Building Society, forerunner of today's mighty HBOS, stamped the town's name on the map like nothing else.

Building societies were originally temporary organisations: self-help clubs which ceased to exist once each of the members had paid off their mortgage.

From these evolved the first 'permanent' building societies.

The Halifax was one of these early permanent societies. However, its roots date back to the Loyal Georgean Society, formed in Halifax on 3 February, 1779. It was established by a group of 50 men from the town, who met at the 'Sign of the Church' and formed themselves into a mutual help society under the presidency of one James Green. The Society had its headquarters in the Old Cock Inn, where the Halifax Permanent Building Society was later formed.

The Loyal Georgean lent money to members to help them build themselves homes. Its largest enterprise was a row of houses, no longer in existence, in St James's Road. But building homes did not prove profitable, so the Loyal Georgean Society gave up the practice.

Many of its members, however, saw an opportunity. John Fisher, the Halifax's first President, and also John Edwards, Joseph Charlton and William Walsh, who were among the first Directors, were all former members of the Loyal Georgean who promoted the establishment of the Halifax Permanent.

A few 'permanent' societies already existed in other northern towns, successfully lending the savings of people who had homes to those who needed homes. The first meeting of the Halifax Permanent Benefit Building Society took place in the Oak Room at the Old Cock Inn in 1852. The man who recorded the minutes of the proceedings in an old school exercise book could little have dreamed that the Society would eventually become the biggest in the world.

Headquarters was a shop in Halifax's Old Market, rented for £10 a year. Jonas Dearnley Taylor was

Left and above right: A 1930s (left) and 1940s view of Permanent buildings. Built in 1921, the former head office of the Halifax Building Society. Below left: Sir Enoch Hill, the man credited with masterminding the society's expansion in the early part of the twentieth century. Below: This 1920s picture of the counter area in the head office is in marked contrast to the modern, relaxed layout of today's typical Halifax branch. Bottom right: The Leeds Permanent building society head office on Park Lane, circa 1930. The merger of two societies in 1995 paved the way for flotation.

In 1928, the Halifax Permanent Benefit Building Society and the Halifax Equitable merged to form the Halifax Building Society. With assets of £47 million it was five times larger than its nearest rival.

Enoch Hill was a driving force behind the Society's expansion, and whenever a new branch opened he made it a special occasion, with a party and important local people as guests. Celebrations were particularly extravagant when the first Halifax office opened in London, in 1924.

On the 50th anniversary of the London opening, the Society was invited to take part in the Lord Mayor of London's parade. The theme that year was 'children' so the Halifax had a float based on nursery rhyme characters. Staff working in the Society's City Offices made their own costumes. The text of the various nursery rhymes decorated the float, the words slightly changed to illustrate the benefits of being a member of the Halifax! Nowadays, new offices are opened without so much fuss. Enoch Hill, however, was knighted for his sterling efforts, original ideas and other services to the Society. More recently, Jim Birrell, Halifax Chief Executive in the late 1980s and early 1990s was also knighted in recognition of his efforts to promote home ownership in the UK.

Headquarters in Commercial Street served the Halifax well for over 50 years, and during this time assets rose to over £3 billion.

appointed as Secretary and kept that position for almost half a century. He devoted his life to making home-ownership a possibility for as many people as possible.

Business burgeoned. In 1853 the first subscription meeting was held. A subscription was expected from both investors and borrowers as a regular installment towards a share in the society.

Outside the town three branches were established within the first year: Sowerby Bridge, Thornton and Queenshead (now Queensbury). In 1862 a branch opened in Huddersfield.

By 1863 the society had to restrict the number of mortgages for the first, but not the last time, because of high interest rates and an increase in the demand for loans. By 1885, the Halifax had the largest reserves of all the Yorkshire building societies. In 1888 'paid up shares' were offered for the first time to investing members who had completed payment on their subscription shares and who wanted to continue their membership.

In the early days, the Society employed men to work for it as agents in the areas where they lived. They called at people's homes to collect funds. By the late 1890s, the agents all had offices where customers brought business to them. There were 50 of these agencies by 1903 when, on the death of Jonas Taylor, Mr Enoch Hill became Secretary.

The Halifax Permanent had more accounts than any other building society by 1905; and by 1913 its assets exceeded £3 million – also more than any other society. Remarkably the second largest building society was based in Halifax too; it seemed logical that the two societies should merge.

However more space was required and the site of the current diamond-shaped building in Trinity Road became available. Work began in 1969 on the old Ramsdens Brewery site and the Society moved there in 1973.

The new Head Office was officially opened by Her Majesty the Queen in 1974. The new building won several design awards, but not all local people were impressed. It did not, they claimed, fit in with the Victorian buildings that surrounded it. However, over time, most doubters come round as it became more familiar, and it is now widely viewed as a building ahead of its time and has become a well-known landmark.

The Head Office site contains many surprises, and indeed there is as much space below ground as there is above. A huge vault, nearly 50 feet below street level is known as Deed Safe and contains all the title deeds to the properties bought with a Halifax mortgage. Title deeds to over one fifth of the UK's housing market are stored, encased in concrete and protected by the latest safety and security devices. The filing is nowadays done by computer, and the vault is linked to the Deeds Department three floors above the ground, by bright red conveyors. There is capacity for almost three million packets of title deeds in the vault, so a new vault will not be required in the immediate future.

In 1988, the Head Office complex was extended still further when a new six-floor office block was built on the adjacent site of the former Collinsons tea and coffee warehouse.

It was decided in the 1980s that the Halifax would need a purpose-built data centre to enter the 1990s with confidence. Built in 1989 the purpose-built centre, on the outskirts of Halifax, on the site of an old rhubarb field at Copley, would house computers and digital communications equipment. At any one time the centre was controlling over 30,000 workstations throughout the Halifax's branch network as well as having telecommunication links with almost every country in the world.

During the 1980s the expansion of the organisation continued apace. In 1980, the Halifax gave its one millionth mortgage and its assets topped £10 billion. By 1996 the Halifax had 20 million accounts whilst its assets exceeded £115 billion.

Building societies had to change and adapt due to the increased competition, mainly from the banks. In November 1994, the Halifax made the historic announcement that it was to merge with the Leeds Permanent Building Society (then the fifth largest building society) and then to convert to a public limited company. Not only did this involve the biggest building society merger in UK history, but it was then followed by the largest extension of share ownership ever witnessed in the UK.

The whole process was a gigantic logistical operation, masterminded by a small team in Halifax ably supported by the help of the thousands of Halifax staff throughout the country. The merger of the two Societies took place on Yorkshire Day, 1 August 1995. Clerical Medical became part of the Halifax Group in the following year.

Over 97% of Halifax BuildingSociety's members had voted in favour of changing the Society's status. Shares were issued to over 7 million qualifying members. Over 20 million individual accounts were checked to ensure members received their correct share entitlement. Over 8 million members received on average £2,300 of the total £19 billion share distribution. The mailing of information about conversion was the single largest mailing ever undertaken by the Royal Mail, involving some 32 million items in over 8 million packs.

Conversion to a plc came on 2 June, 1997. The organisation became the 8th largest company in the UK with a new name, simply: The Halifax.

The new 'Halifax' offered an extensive range of products and services, ranging from savings schemes for children, a

Top left: *A 1960s view of the Commercial Street headquarters.* **Remaining pictures:** *Various stages of construction of the new Trinity Road diamond shaped head office.*

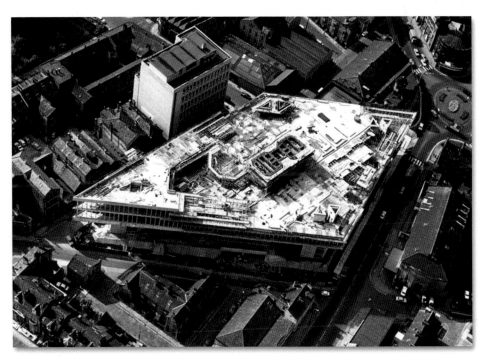

Acquisition of Birmingham Midshires was completed in April the following year, and Halifax Group plc, a parent holding company was created.

More expansion followed. On 22 March 2000 Halifax conditionally acquired 60% of the shares held by Prudential in St James Place Capital. Exactly three months later Halifax Group plc purchased the UK retail credit card business of Bank One.

The launch of a completely new stand-alone bank, Intelligent Finance, in October 2000 saw a revolutionary new banking proposition being offered to customers, allowing them to benefit by connecting any combination of accounts for interest purposes, including their mortgage, credit card, personal loan, savings and current account. Customers could also now conduct their banking via the telephone, e-mail, and the Internet and access balance information on WAP

comprehensive range of banking products as well as a range of savings accounts for people of all ages, both on and offshore. The Halifax continued to be the UK's largest mortgage lender whilst developing its offshore activities in Jersey and the Isle of Man which act as bases for British expatriates. The Halifax also sought to extend its services in other European markets, for example through a Spanish subsidiary, Banco Halifax Hispania, based in Madrid, Seville and Barcelona.

More change would follow. Expresscash - an account for 11-15 year olds – saw almost 60,000 accounts opened by the end of 1997.

On 11 December, 1998, the investing and borrowing members of Birmingham Midshires Building Society gave their overwhelming approval for Birmingham Midshires to be acquired by the Halifax.

telephones. Over 1,400 call centre, administration, sales and support staff were recruited and trained.

By the end of 2000 Intelligent Finance received approximately 82,000 account applications, including 28,000 current account and 21,000 credit card applications. Daily applications were around 2,300, and approved borrowing around £1bn.

The Halifax could boast it had more customers than any other UK bank, that is was the UK's largest provider of mortgages, and the market leader in UK household savings.

On 4 May, 2001, the Boards of both Halifax and Bank of Scotland announced that they had agreed to a merger, to become effective on 10 September, 2001.

Launched as 'The New Force in British banking', HBOS plc - the Halifax Bank of Scotland - created a major new competitor in the UK financial services market. Its combined assets, expertise and customer base allowed it to compete with the 'Big Four' clearing banks and to challenge the status quo.

The existing, distinctive, brands (Halifax, Bank of Scotland, Clerical Medical, and Birmingham Midshires) were retained, but the company was structured upon four separate customer divisions – Retail Banking, Business Banking, Corporate Banking and Insurance and Investment.

In 2002 HBOS had over two and half million shareholders, with assets of £355 billion, and a workforce of some 60,000. It had secured a 29% share of net mortgage lending and was the number one savings institution in the UK. By April 2004, HBOS plc had assets of £408 billion and announced pre-tax profits of £3.8 billion.

Overseas, Halifax's Spanish subsidiary, Banco Halifax Hispania, announced that it would open seven additional branches in Spain throughout 2005.

On 1 March, 2006, the Halifax announced that it would be opening one hundred new branches in the south of England in the next five years. The branch opening programme, the biggest of its kind in the UK banking sector for many years, would be the largest network expansion by the Halifax since the 1970s.

Meanwhile technology moves on. The Halifax issued its first 'contactless' debit cards on Monday, 12 November, 2007. The new Visa payWave debit cards, initially issued to around 25,000 existing customers, allows users to pay for low-cost items simply by waving a plastic card over a scanner.

Today the presence of one of the UK's top ten companies in Halifax town centre continues to be a daily source of not only employment but also of immense local pride.

Pictures: *A range of photographs dating from the completion of the award winning Trinity Road head office in 1973 to the present day.*

Parkinson-Spencer Refractories - Hot Stuff!

refractories was to be found in only two locations: at Stourbridge in the West Midlands, and around Halifax.

The firm's founder Caleb Spencer was born in 1766. He was apprenticed to a local farmer, but later ran the Dog & Gun Inn at Oxenhope which had rights to the nearby seam of clay. His daughter married David Parkinson, who made his living from coal, clay, stone and the land. By the middle of the 19th century

A local business with a world-class reputation in the production of quality products for the glass industry is now in its third century of manufacture from its premises in Holmfield, Halifax. Parkinson-Spencer Refractories has been a family-run business for seven generations. From 1800 to the present day fireclay, mined from the deposits owned by the firm, has been supplied, in various forms, to the glass industry throughout the world.

At one time there were many local firms which utilised the local clays, manufacturing firebricks, sanitaryware and clay pipes: today PSR is one of only a small number of survivors.

During the course of the Industrial Revolution it gradually became evident that the best quality clay for making glassworks

Top left: *A 1940s view of the factory.* **Above:** *Glass melting pots storage room in 1940.* **Below:** *Early surface grinding of refractory blocks.*

the two families concentrated increasingly on their clay and fire-brick manufacturing business, trading under the name of Parkinson & Spencer. By the end of the century the seam of clay they had been mining was nearing exhaustion so the firm moved to Holmfield.

The First World War was a catalyst for change. The adoption of a more scientific approach to the manufacturing process contributed to a much-needed increase in efficiency and cost-effectiveness. Caleb Parkinson, the fourth generation of the founding family, set about producing refractory blocks for glass production which could withstand the increasingly high temperatures demanded by the latest furnaces for which Stourbridge clay was less suitable.

A family dispute over the expectation that a cousin, Harry Newton, would be given a job in the firm led to a split in the firm, and to the brothers Caleb and Spencer Parkinson forming the limited company Parkinson & Spencer Ltd in 1921.

In the 1920s the firm adopted new methods of ramming, slip-casting and vacuum slip-casting, and worked constantly to improve the composition of its clay pots, subjecting them to frequent analysis and adopting the analyst's recommendations. The business received a substantial boost when a tariff was introduced on imported glass. During the

1930s the firm started to export its products overseas, to Spain, South Africa, New Zealand, Australia, Greece, Norway, India and Italy, and even Argentina.

The outbreak of war in September 1939 was the beginning of a period of great difficulties. There were many orders, but a large number of workers joined the forces. The firm also had difficulty complying with blackout regulations since the coal-fired kilns threw out flames from the chimneys when they were being stoked up. To disguise the kiln a loose wooden structure was placed every night round the fires. This created appalling working conditions for the kiln stokers. As well as shortage of materials, spare parts, and labour, the industry also came under central state control from August 1941.

Women were recruited to take the place of men, and towards the end of the war the firm took on prisoners of war. By November 1944 the POWs accounted for half the workforce. The strain took its toll on Spencer Parkinson, who in March 1945 was advised by his doctor to retire, though he remained a director until his death that October. Fellow Director, Doris Spencer, died around the same time and was replaced by Harry Newton whose hopes for a job had caused the dissolution of the original firm. Since then he had worked for a subsidiary of ICI, as the director of a soda ash factory in

Top left: Clay mining in Shibden Valley. **Above:** *Manufacture of glass pot in the 1940s.* **Below:** *Grinding refractory blocks circa 1940.*

South Africa. He would prove a valuable resource until his death in 1970.

In September 1945 Caleb Parkinson's son, Henry had joined the firm. He had graduated from Sheffield University in 1943 and then spent two years with ICI. Henry joined the board in 1946.

After the end of the Second World War there was still a serious shortage of materials. Sillimanite, an important raw material, was very scarce until 1949; in the previous year the firm at times had barely enough to operate one day a week. Strikes by miners and the appalling winter of 1947, also made the supply of coal erratic. Plans for modernising the firm's buildings and plant however, were delayed because they were still subject to the wartime system of licensing. In 1947 after suffering much due to unreliable supplies of coal, the firm switched to oil-fired kilns. Bringing coal-fired kilns up to the required temperature, evenly spread throughout the kiln had been an art. Oil-fired kilns were much easier to operate and the skill of the kiln-stokers was consequently lost.

The company introduced many new working practices during the years immediately following the end of the war, a result of Henry Parkinson's tour of the refractory industry in the USA. By 1954 the firm was making 550 glass melting pots per year. Pot making was becoming an increasingly rare skill. The process was so closely guarded that senior pot makers often refused to carry on working if someone entered the room. A modern pot-making workshop in which the temperature and humidity were thermostatically controlled to ensure the clay could dry evenly enabled a skilled pot-maker to produce a dozen pots a month. Each pot, holding up to three-quarters of a ton of molten glass was expected to last anything above three months in production. Melting temperatures of 1,350 deg C were now 100 deg C higher than thirty years previously. A further significant step was taken by the company in 1957 when it decided to replace the old intermittent kilns with a new continuous tunnel kiln; this was cheaper to install and operate than the older kilns. The cost was £60,000, and purchased mainly with a preferential loan from the Ministry of Fuel and Power. It was ideally suited to the firm's product range at the time. It took five kiln cars carrying up to five tons of refractory blocks every other day, operating on a three-week cycle.

The 1960s saw a considerable expansion of the export business after Henry Parkinson became Managing Director in 1960. In-house research and development work was undertaken to improve sillimanite and mullite blocks. A

Top left: A 1946 tipper for transporting clay. ***Above:*** Early brochures. ***Below:*** Loading refractory blocks by hand.

licence agreement made with the Hartford Empire Corporation, known under the Emhart name, created the chance for the company to supply numerous glass-making firms world-wide. As a result, export sales increased to seventy per cent of total sales by the end of 1985.

David Parkinson, Henry's son, the seventh generation of the family to enter the business, joined the Board of Directors in 1976. At that time it was felt that a change of name would be beneficial and the company was renamed Parkinson-Spencer Refractories Ltd, becoming universally known as PSR. By the close of the 1980s, exports accounted for 78 per cent of turnover and the company's four main product lines, feeder expendables, furnace blocks, forehearth refractories and glasshouse pots all contributed equally to sales. Computers came to the company in the early 1980s, as well as the realisation of the need to meet internationally recognised quality standards. Many changes to the firm's production techniques were necessary before the company was granted the quality assurance standard of BS5750/ISO9002 in 1993.

The years since 1990 have seen radical changes in PSR's product range. The use of glasshouse pots for the melting of glass has been gradually superseded by newer technologies, though with

PSR left as the only UK source, and one of the few world sources, for this unique product. The most significant change of direction however, has been the shift into engineered products complimentary to the company's mainstream refractory products. Primarily used in the glass container manufacturing industry, but also to be found in the tableware, lighting and TV glass industries, PSR's forehearth systems combine a knowledge and experience in the manufacture of special refractory shapes with the complex sciences of glass thermal conditioning. That evolution has transformed the company into one that is internationally renowned for advanced glass conditioning systems.

The company has prospered by producing quality products and meeting change with innovation. These principles have stood PSR in good stead for over two centuries and will continue to do so in the future.

Top left: A moving hood kiln, 2006. *Above:* Modern refractory grinding. *Below:* A 2006 view of Parkinson - Spencer Refractories Ltd's Holmfield factory.

Off to Market

Halifax Borough Market is probably the finest Victorian Market building in the whole of Britain. The grade A Listed Building is of enormous architectural and historical interest.

Prior to 1790, the site of the Halifax market was adjacent to the Union Cross public house, still recalled in the adjacent street names, Corn Market, Old Market and Swine Market.

In 1790, the old market was superseded by The New Market, sited between Market Street and Southgate, directly opposite the Old Cock Inn. It appears to have been established in an effort to impose more order upon the frequently obstructive stalls and standings. In 1810 a Parliamentary Act was secured to permit closer regulation of its affairs. A joint stock company was capitalised at £3,000, divided into £50 shares, to fund land purchase and premises.

The trustees were empowered to prohibit the slaughtering of livestock except in recognised slaughterhouses or 'shambles', and also the setting up of any shops or stalls in the footpaths or highways. Cow Green, however, would long remain an open cattle market.

By 1823, the New Market was formally established beginning the process of moving away from the open-air stalls and 'shambles'. John Crabtree described it in his Concise History of the Parish and Vicarage of Halifax:

The market place is separated from Southgate by iron palisades. The west end adjoining this street is an open square in the centre whereof stands an ornamental pillar, serving the useful purpose of a pump and a lamp post. The market buildings are of red brick. A building extends, from the centre of the East side of the square to the bottom of the market. forming

a double row of shops and divides the market place into two compartments. The shops on both sides of the square and on the north side of the market together with all the shops in the centre building are occupied as a shambles. The shops on the south side have rooms above them and are occupied as dwellings. All the shops are fronted by a colonnade. The southern compartment of the market is considerably broader than the other and in the centre thereof is a covered shed for the erection of standings wherein are sold miscellaneous articles. In this compartment are the fish, fruit and vegetable markets. A broad colonnade projecting from the centre building is used by the country people for the sale of butter, eggs and cheese. The vacant spaces on market days are occupied by temporary stalls. At the bottom of the market place are large and convenient slaughterhouses under proper regulations as regards their cleanliness.

A Development Act of 1853 empowered the Corporation to purchase the markets and market rights from the market company for of £7,700.

Fifteen years later, the Corporation also acquired the Piece Hall and converted it into a wholesale market to service the retail New Market. In this form, the Piece Hall reopened in 1871. Within the next ten years, a covered cattle shed and market replaced the open-air shambles. It had been unofficially known as the Feasting Shed but in January 1889 the Markets Committee resolved to rename it the Lower Market. As such it survived until 1968.

In 1884 an Improvement Committee decided to carry out a scheme for widening Southgate and Old Market. Since the market was Corporation property, they chose to site the new market nearby. As a result Southgate became 'A serviceable road of 50 feet width in place of a narrow street of less than half that width'.

Top left: Early market trading at the Old Market area.
Left: The Duke and Duchess of York visiting the Borough Market in 1896. The Duke later became King George V.
*Above: Southgate at the turn of the 20th century. **Below:** An early view of Market Arcade and Old Market.*

At the meeting of the Markets and Fairs Committee on 20 August, 1890, it was resolved that that the markets between Southgate and Market Street should be reconstructed.

On 4 June, 1891 the Markets and Fairs Committee selected plans submitted to it under the non-de-plume of 'Auld Lang Syne' by Leeming and Leeming of London. Leeming and Leeming were, in fact, Joseph and John Leeming, they were both born in Halifax and originally practiced in Northgate. The total cost was expected to be £112,028. The Leemings' plans allowed for 43 butchers' shops, 20 small shops and 33 stalls, perimeter shops on Market Street and Southgate, and 22 dwellings.

To finance the scheme the Council borrowed £50,000 from the Local Government Board (a Government body empowered to grant loans for municipal buildings). Most of the work was given to local firms.

The Local Government Board held an enquiry on 22 March, 1895 resulting in another loan of £33,000, taking costs to nearly £120,000. The architects blamed the increase on the fair wages clause which raised prices from 21/2d to 41/4d per cubic foot. Finally the building was ready for its official opening in July, 1896.

Today the first thing that is immediately obvious is the sloping site upon which the market is built. But there are no steps to inconvenience customers, a fact of some importance in these days of concern for the disabled. The Central Hall has an octagonal dome rising to 60 feet above floor level and supported on decorative cast iron pillars, below the large ornamental clock can be seen from almost any position. Aisles were 10 feet wide when the market originally opened but many alterations have resulted in some narrower aisles. The total area of the building

*Top: A view down Albion Street which show some of the fresh fish merchants shops which have characterised the area for over a century. **Below:** Market Street. The photograph captures the impressive Victorian architecture of the exterior of the Market Hall.*

covers some 5,800 square metres with internal retail space of 2,125 square metres.

In 1896 the annual rental for shops varied between £13.00 and £36.00. Stalls were on a weekly rental at half a crown (2 shillings and 6 pence) to 8 shillings. The shops in the arcades were rented at £100.00 per year. In addition to the shops in the arcade leading into Russell Street, the outer shell of the market provides a large number of shops facing outwards into Southgate, Russell Street, Market Street and Albion Street.

The Fish Market was originally within the Hall proper, although partitioned off, and was entered by way of one of the arcades - the Albany. However, after a few years the Fish Market was moved to shops fronting on to Albion Street. During the passage of time the majority of the original shop fronts have been replaced but, many have been restored to look like the Victorian originals. The Markets Service now encourages all tenants to restore their selling areas sympathetically to the original design.

The shops facing into Southgate and Market Street had living accommodation consisting of a kitchen and parlour on the first

floor, bedroom and toilet on the second floor and two attic bedrooms. These homes looked out over a balcony and, because tradesmen lived over the shop, there was also direct access from the shops below. The Market Inspector was provided with on-site living quarters on the Albion Street elevation, the living room window looking directly into the market. This accommodation is now used as the Market Undertakings General Office.

The rooms above Southgate are now used as showrooms or storage. In Market Street the accommodation still exists but no longer connects with the shops below.

In the original market complex there were three public houses in Market Street, plus the Boars Head (which remained a public house until acquired by Bradford and Bingley Building Society in 1992) in Southgate. A replacement for the former 'Peacock Hotel' was incorporated at the corner of Albion Street and

Market Street and also named the 'Peacock'.

The licence for the new Peacock was held by the Corporation. The pub was replaced by the present shop and showrooms in the 1960s. At the other end of the market block was the 'Saddle' demolished in the mid-1960s and replaced by a building first designed as a supermarket for Liptons and now occupied by sports retailers JJB Sports. The third Market Street pub was the 'Wheatsheaf', a fact commemorated by a sculptured wheatsheaf incorporated into the stone work half way up the building: the pub has since been renamed 'Portman and Pickles' after the actor Eric Portman and broadcaster Wilfred Pickles, both Halifax men.

The building design provided eight access points to the market hall, each of which was furbished with three pairs of heavy wooden swing doors, constructed of red pine. In 2005 new automatic sliding doors where installed at seven entrances. Only the Arcade entrance now preserves the memory of what, for over a century, had been one of the prominent features of the market.

Left and top: Inside Halifax Borough Market where a friendly smile and a kind word are the norm. Below: A Fun Day, one of the many events organised by the Borough Market Tenants Association and members of Calderdale MBC's Market Committee.

Crossley Heath School
Progress and a Proud Heritage

One of Halifax's landmark buildings, Crossley Heath School, with its imposing Mansard roofline, has dominated the views across Savile Park for over 140 years. On winter mornings, when the parkland is blanketed in mist, the vast building appears to emerge as if from another age.

Built of local stone, the school buildings are sited in a prominent position at the north east corner of Savile Park between Skircoat Moor Road and Free School Lane, commanding a prime position in views up and across the park. The main blocks have two main storeys with gable windows to the third storey. The higher corner pavilions have steeply sloping blue slate roofs with inset windows and decorative cast iron rail and finial detailing. The elaborate entrance tower to the centre of the south east front

rises to a clock, cupola and weather vane. From the west the more utilitarian blocks and later additions can be seen above a high stone boundary wall.

Today, between bells for lessons, students walk corridors that were initially glimpsed by James Labron Plint, the very first boy to arrive at what was then the Crossley Orphan Home when it opened in 1864.

Art lessons now take place where years before there were dormitories where children once slept in iron-framed beds, their day clothes tucked into wire baskets before they went to sleep.

Students today play badminton and volleyball in a gym which originally housed the orphanage joiners' workshop. At lunchtimes diners now choose their lunches and sit to chat where blackboards once stood in 'glasshouse' classrooms of the turn of the last century.

The history and architecture of what is now the Crossley Heath School is an enduring legacy of a philanthropic family, a gift treasured and handed on by each generation to the next, and one which those who are fortunate to have studied and worked there are justly proud to be a part.

Top left: *A 19th century view of the Orphan Home and School for Boys and Girls.* **Left:** *A delightful photograph from 1866 when the school took in orphans from the surrounding areas. Mr Oliver and Mrs Smith are pictured outside the main entrance with their pupils.* **Above:** *Francis, John and Joseph Crossley.*

The ornamental clock tower housed a hand-wound, flat bed clock driven by massive weights suspended into the cellar of the building (the clock is still hand-wound to this day, an honour given to Sixth Form students whose names are chalked inside the tower dating from as far back as 1889).

An endowment fund was established to finance the ongoing costs of running the orphanage: other local benefactors, including the industrialist Sir Titus Salt, and the Brighouse mill owner Thomas Omerod, added to the fund. In 1887 a Lancastrian yarn merchant, Thomas Porter, who had no connection with Halifax and never set foot in the building, made an endowment of £50,000 with the condition that his name be added to the orphanage. His generosity meant that what now became the Crossley and Porter Orphan Home and School would continue to care for around 250 children until the beginning of the First World War.

Francis, John and Joseph Crossley were the respected, hard working and chapel-going sons of John Crossley senior, a weaver-turned-foreman who had first leased a small mill at Dean Clough in 1802.

As his business grew, pioneering techniques in steam-driven looms placed the brothers at the centre of a carpet weaving empire which would eventually stretch across Europe and America.

The wealth this brought enabled the brothers to turn their hand to public works and, among commissions for almshouses, a church and a park, by 1861 they had resolved to build an Orphan Home and School for Boys and Girls in Halifax.

Designed by John Hogg and modelled on architecture of the reign of King James I, 'with a mixture of the Italian style', building of the Orphanage began on land belonging to John Crossley, "eight acres, two roods and eight perches", on Skircoat Moor. By the time the building was completed in 1864, construction costs had amounted to £56,000 and included accommodation for a planned 400 orphans. The building included a vast, almost industrial-sized laundry, a tailors' room for sewing and mending, a sick room, swimming baths, dormitories and classrooms.

By 1895, according to a contemporary directory, 'the Orphanage and School liberally feeds, clothes and educates from 200 to 300 children, most of whom contribute between £5.00 and £10.00 per annum as evidence of good faith and an acknowledgement of the benefits received'.

Boys and girls were taught separately, though they mixed on social occasions and in the playground. They studied arithmetic, reading, writing and scripture as well as geography, basic science, singing and drawing. The more able boys were instructed in Latin, algebra and geometry,

Top left: The six assistant masters pictured in 1892 on the girls' terrace. Centre: The ornamental clock tower. Below: The hooped rugby jerseys of the 1889-90 Crossley and Porter rugby team in the year the boys received their first proper boots to play in, replacing their heavy, clasp-fastened school shoes. The bearded gentleman in the background is Mr William Barber, Principal of the orphanage from 1872 to 1910.

The fine gardens were designed and laid out by Charles Kershaw, a Brighouse gardener who also created and transformed the gardens at the Rydings as well as several other houses in the district.

The orphanage was open to any fatherless child of either sex, and children between the ages of two and ten years of age were admitted from all over Britain. In the first 25 years, 1,100 entered, receiving free board and lodging, clothing and education with the girls remaining until age of 17 and the boys until they were apprenticed at 15.

whereas girls' education had originally tended to emphasise the practical crafts of needlework and 'household service'. When a new principal, William Barber, joined the school in 1872, the curriculum was broadened for girls, and within a few years they were taking examinations in animal physiology, physical geography and botany.

A digitally-recovered version of an original wax-cylinder recording of Mr Barber reading aloud from passages of Shakespeare and Robert Burns can be found on the School's website today.

As numbers of orphans grew so did the number of staff: in 1892 there were six assistant masters in addition to a similar number of resident lady teachers. And soon there were also more than 30 domestic staff on site.

The Education Act of 1918 recognised Crossley and Porter as a grant earning school, approved by the Board of Education. The Act simultaneously raised the school leaving age to 14 and enabled the admission of fee-paying day pupils in addition to the orphans already receiving their education there as boarders.

Building on tradition - looking to the future

By 1925, the numbers of boarders had declined to 125 whilst the numbers of day pupils had reached

175. Continuing educational reform during the Second World War years between 1939 and 1945 brought many changes, including, finally, the end of boarding at the school. Despite this, Crossley and Porter continued to flourish and expand. The school became voluntary-controlled in 1945, and then fully co-educational under the management of a single Head in 1968.

1985 saw the merger of the neighbouring 400-year-old Heath Grammar School with Crossley and Porter.

Heath Grammar School in Free School Lane, which had also been known as the Halifax Free School, or the Free Grammar School of Queen Elizabeth, was founded by the vicar of Halifax, Dr John Favour, in 1600.

Top left: The girls' dormitory dating from the early 1900s. *Left:* The school laundry room. *Above:* Crossley & Porter Orphan Home and School in 1925. *Below:* An aerial view taken from Wainhouse Tower in 1928 shows the expanding school building which by then housed a new laundry and a two-storey extension for the girls' Headmistress. 'Fives' courts were under construction (by the open section of the shed on the left) which stood until 2002. In the background, the white tents of the Yorkshire Show are seen covering the expanse of Savile Park as they do each summer today.

A World Class Education

The school achieves excellent academic results year after year which place it among the top state schools in the country. Crossley Heath was named a Beacon school when that scheme was first established, allowing it to share its good practice with other schools in the locality. Today, as a Language College, teachers continue to support local primary schools in their language teaching, and classes also run after school which are open to all members of the community.

The School has received many awards in recent years including Investor in People, the Arts Council's 'Artsmark', the Sports Council's 'Sportsmark', the Healthy Schools Award and the International Schools Award. Following an excellent Ofsted report in 2006, Crossley Heath's ongoing success was recognised in its designation as a High Performing

The schools came together on a single site three years after their merger under the name of Crossley Heath. In 1991 the school once again left local authority control to become grant-maintained.

Today, The Crossley Heath School continues to go from strength to strength. Two years after the appointment of Headteacher Helen Gaunt in 2001, it achieved Specialist School status as a designated Language College. A new wing containing the most modern accommodation and IT facilities for language teaching was opened by the Mayor and Chair of Governors, Mrs Joan Tidswell. Since then, the school has extended into another purpose-built wing which houses five specialist classrooms for DT, Textiles and Food. Maths suites and other classrooms have been refurbished within the main school building, where interactive whiteboards and wi-fi networks are now the order of the day

Specialist School. Since then it has also received the rare accolade of achieving a second specialism, this time in Leadership Development.

As well as academic excellence, Crossley Heath regularly receives public recognition for the achievement of its students on a range of fronts. Pupils take part in many extra curricular activities including a wide range of sports, drama, music, dance, debating, community leadership, Young Enterprise and Duke of Edinburgh schemes. Their continued success on so many fronts reflects the high aspirations which the school nurtures in its students, underpinned by its strong traditions and values.

Top left: A new wing containing the most modern accommodation and IT facilities for language teaching opened by the Mayor and Chair of Governors, Mrs Joan Tidswell (left). Above: 115 years since orphanage boys got their first boots, a jubilant Crossley Heath First XV win the coveted Daily Mail Vase at Twickenham in 2005. Left: Headteacher Helen Gaunt pictured with pupils in 2008.

RSA - A Halifax Firm Delivering World Class Brands

The RSA Group (formerly Royal & SunAlliance Insurance Group) currently employs 1,000 staff at Dean Clough, in Halifax. Those staff are mainly involved in servicing RSA's personal insurance business.

Insurance has been around for a very long time. As early as 600 AD The Greeks and Romans had health and life insurance organised through benevolent societies. The societies cared for the families and paid funeral expenses of members on their deaths.

England's trade guilds in the Middle Ages served a similar purpose to their classical predecessors. Before insurance companies were established in the late 17th century, 'friendly societies' already existed in England, in which people paid money to a general sum that could be used for emergencies. Some Friendly Societies still exist.

Separate insurance contracts were invented in Genoa in the 14th century, as were insurance pools backed by pledges of land. These new insurance contracts allowed insurance to be separated from investment, a separation of roles that first proved useful in marine insurance.

Insurance as we typically know it today can be traced to the Great Fire of London. The fire of 1666 destroyed 13,200 houses. In the aftermath of that conflagration, Nicholas Barbon opened an office to insure buildings. In 1680 Barbon established England's first fire insurance company, 'The Fire Office' to insure brick and frame homes.

As the seventeenth century drew to a close, London's growing importance as a centre for international trade led increasing demand for marine insurance. In the late 1680s Edward Lloyd opened a coffee house that became a popular haunt of ship owners, merchants, and ships' captains. The venue became an excellent source of the latest shipping news. It also became the meeting place for people wanting to take out insurance on ships and their cargoes, and those willing to sell such insurance.

Top left: This picture portrays the original house 'North Park', which lies to one corner of People's Park. The house and its gardens were occupied by the offices of Bradford-Pennine Insurance until the mid-1990s. The picture was reproduced for a commemorative plate in 1987 when motor insurance policies exceeded one million in number. *Left: Dean Clough, current home of RSA since 1944. This picture was taken circa 1900. Above:* Above: A 'Firemark'. These were used in the 17th and 18th centuries. Before the days of street names and numbers, insurance company Firemarks were attached to the outsides of buildings insured by them. Over time, the 'marks' acquired a subsidiary social function in that having insurance, and of course the choice of insurer, gave an indication of the owner's standing in society.

RSA has had a presence in Halifax since 1944 when a Halifax insurance broker established the Pennine Insurance Company to transact all types of insurance with the exception of life insurance.

The penultimate year of the Second World War, with petrol rationing still very much in force, was not an obviously propitious time to establish a new insurance business. Very soon after the war however, private car insurance became the specialist area of the company.

Cars first arrived on Britain's roads at the very end of the Victorian era. For many years there were no driving tests, nor any requirements for insurance. Motor insurance did exist, but it was not compulsory and few drivers were covered. Due to the poor standards of driving skills, little road discipline, faster vehicles and ever increasing numbers accidents soon became a common sight on Britain's roads.

Many motorists who had spent large sums on buying their own vehicles were now finding themselves out of pocket if their vehicles were damaged or destroyed. And on the other side of the equation was the total lack of compensation for innocent victims involved in these road traffic accidents. This situation was addressed by Parliament when it passed the first Road Traffic Act in 1930.

Amongst its other provisions the Road Traffic Act made it compulsory for vehicle owners and drivers to be insured for their liability for injury or death to third parties whilst their vehicle was being used on a public road.

In 1959, fifteen years after Pennine Insurance had been founded in Halifax, Bradford Insurance was founded as a diversification of the interests of the Tulketh Textile Group. Originally intended to build a sound fire and accident portfolio centred on the Tulketh Headquarters at Peckover Street, Bradford, it rapidly began to win a competitive reputation in the life and motor insurance markets.

Both Bradford Insurance and Pennine Insurance began to specialise in providing motor insurance and had much in common, so the advantages of amalgamation became increasingly obvious. Even more than 40 years ago the problem of high operational expenses suffered by smaller companies was evident, and it is not surprising that both Bradford Insurance and Pennine insurance were searching for the same economies.

*Top: Dean Clough. Since this picture was taken many changes have taken place at Dean Clough. RSA occupies the building in the centre right of the picture. **Above:** A compliment slip dating from the 1970s.*

Negotiations for the merger were completed in 1965 and whilst separate Head Offices were retained for a while, more and more processes were undertaken in Halifax and the premises at North Park (on one corner of People's Park) eventually became the head office of the newly formed Bradford-Pennine Insurance Company.

Bradford-Pennine dedicated itself to business produced by insurance brokers and in 1965 dealt with 2,500 brokers, all of whom were authorised to sell motor insurance on a full credit basis. Policyholders of the company grew from 175,000 in 1965 to 257,000 in 1973 but the next few years were ones of intense activity for Bradford-Pennine with the number of policyholders growing to 700,000, and premium income growing fourfold to £31m. A number of changes were introduced to accommodate the expansion of the company including the centralisation of a dedicated claims office dealing with third party claims leaving the staff in the branch offices free to concentrate on the best possible service to the policyholder.

The growth continued as Bradford-Pennine became a subsidiary of the Phoenix Group, providing the company with appropriate capital to continue its expansion and achieve increasing economies of scale.

In August 1984 the Phoenix Group merged with SunAlliance, but Bradford-Pennine was largely unaffected operationally, although soon after many of the staff were moved to premises in the newly-refurbished offices at Bowling Mill, Dean Clough.

The company commemorated the sale of its one millionth motor insurance policy in 1987 by giving a special plate to all of its staff. The following year the company was awarded best Insurer of the Year by the institute of Insurance Brokers. Dedication to the broker market was further confirmed in 1995 with the merger of the SunAlliance's broker household insurance business based in Oldham, giving the combined operation a greater range of products to offer its broker agents.

By now firmly established as one of the UK's leading motor insurers, there were further major changes around the corner when in 1996 SunAlliance and Royal Insurance merged to create the UK's largest general insurer - Royal & SunAlliance Group.

SunAlliance's origins dated back to the foundation of the Sun Insurance office in London in 1710. Royal & SunAlliance has strong connections with two of Britain's great historic seaports outside of London-Liverpool where Royal Insurance had its roots back in 1845, and Bristol where Phoenix Assurance was established in 1782.

Above: This nostalgic advertisement was run in the 1980s. The shop shown was one of those insured by Bradford Pennine in its infancy. Below: The laying of the foundation stones of the new offices at North Park in the 1970s.

Doubtless it was those seafaring connections that led Royal & SunAlliance to sponsor yachtswoman Tracy Edwards and her all female crew, which on 1st July 1997 set a new record in their catamaran 'Royal & SunAlliance' for the fastest all female crew to sail across the Atlantic. The record was established in nine days, eleven hours and twenty two minutes.

Halifax now became the Headquarters for the enlarged group's Personal Insurance, Broker Division, encompassing Bradford-Pennine and expanding within the Dean Clough premises. The newly merged operation retained its focus on the broker market and now boasted personal insurance premium income of some £450m, generated from over 10,000 brokers and agents selling its motor and household products.

Today Halifax is established as one of RSA's main operating centres and continues to grow on the back of the Group's thriving Affinity business. The Affinity business is based on working with partners who are looking to enhance their own position, or drive additional revenue, by using insurance as a by-product. Typically, this can involve using the partner's brand to sell insurance.

Some of the well-known partners who have their business serviced in Halifax include automotive companies such as Honda, Ford and Toyota as well as Financial Services Intermediaries such as Yorkshire Building Society. The Group has also recently secured a long term partnership with The National Trust, as the provider of motor and home insurance policies to its 3.5 million members.

The success of the Halifax site has been built on the loyalty of the RSA people, the vast majority of whom are local to the town.

Today, RSA is the UK's largest commercial lines insurer with a personal insurance business ranked third largest in the UK, with around 4 million policies in place. UK policies are worth £2,688 million annually.

Internationally the RSA Group employs 22,000 staff and continues to go from strength to strength, with the town of Halifax playing a key role in the Group's success.

Above: When the new offices were completed, Bradford-Pennine were fortunate to have them officially opened by HRH Prince Charles, The Prince of Wales. Below: The reception of the RSA offices in Bowling Mill, Dean Clough, 2008.

Woolshops - 500 years of Commerce

If for nothing else 'Woolshops' in Halifax would be famous as the only street in the country, indeed in the world, with that name. Yet Woolshops is so much more than just a unique name: it is both a reminder of Halifax's distinguished past and a thriving, revitalised, part of its present.

Today Halifax's Woolshops retail district is a paradise for bargain hunters with around 40 well known outlets all centrally-located around an attractive traffic free pedestrian zone. Major high street names exist alongside smaller speciality stores stocking everything from clothes to greeting cards. Convenient adjacent parking makes a shopping experience at The Woolshops a real pleasure. Additionally, the proximity of the bus station further aids those wishing to visit this historic area of Halifax, which was once renowned for the sale of wool, hence the name.

By the 15th Century, Halifax had become a thriving textile town especially known for 'kersey'. Unfortunately, locally grown wool was too coarse for the yarn needed to weave it.

A trade emerged with local wools sold on to areas making stouter, rougher cloths, and Calderdale weavers buying the wool they needed from dealers in Halifax. Woolshops was the area of the town where this trade took place.

The Woolshops area dates back to medieval times, and is mentioned in a 1555 Act of Parliament.

Woolshops was once part of one of the main roads in Halifax. Until the construction of the road over Godley, along what is now Shibden Hall Road, packhorses loaded with goods would approach Halifax from Hipperholme

along the ancient Magna Via, down the narrow setted track from Beacon Hill and over the Hebble stream at Clark Bridge, up Cripplegate and Woolshops to Old Market.

At one time Woolshops was lined with four-storey timber buildings (stone only replaced timber construction towards the end of the 16th century) leading up from the old centre of the town around the parish church. As the name suggests these buildings in Woolshops were shops owned by wool traders, and each building was divided into living accommodation, workshops and warehousing.

At the height of its prosperity this part of town was a centre for foreign merchants, especially from Holland. It is said that in the late 17th century one would have heard almost every European language being spoken here.

The wool trade eventually became more dispersed throughout the town, and in 1779 the Piece Hall opened as a central market for selling cloth.

In the 19th century however, the Woolshops area began a slow decline, as the commercial centre of the town migrated towards Southgate and Commercial Street. The area was still a busy shopping area though, and most things could be bought in Woolshops. There were butchers, newsagents, bootmakers, pawnbrokers and chemists.

A gradual decline continued throughout the 19th and the 20th centuries. By the early decades of the 20th century prior to redevelopment the whole area was a warren of narrow streets, and very much a slum.

In 1931 the south side of Woolshops, now WH Smiths, was renovated in a contemporary style, with imposing towers and a shopping arcade, these towers were later replicated in the present-day centre. As part of that development the road was widened and several buildings pulled down, not least 14 shops and three pubs.

The White Horse Inn and the Old Talbot were pubs in Woolshops which were demolished. The Talbot, said to once

Left: An early 20th century view of the old lower Woolshops.
Below left: A post war bird's eye view of the old Woolshops.
Below: A 1968 view from the bottom end of town looking towards the town centre through the old Woolshops.

have been a haunt of Bramwell Bronte, was replaced with another building but was again demolished to make way for the Woolshops shopping complex in the late 1970s.

In the 1970s many more buildings were demolished ready for redevelopment of the area. Happily the 'Tudor' building at the top of Woolshops remained. Many will recall it then as Paul's Gentlemen's outfitters: today it currently trades as a coffee shop. Also original is the row of shops between Thorntons and Claires' Accessories which are listed buildings.

When, in the 1960s, many British towns were demolishing and rebuilding their centres, there was a plan to do the same in Halifax. Everything between the Parish Church and the Town Hall would have gone. But nothing was done. In 1979 a new Halifax Town Centre redevelopment scheme with indoor mall and bridge to the Piece Hall was rejected by the Secretary of State for the Environment. Many local people saw it as unsympathetic to the adjacent town centre and Piece Hall. The Halifax Civic Trust had taken a lead, publishing a report called "Halifax: The Case for Conservation" and retaining legal representation for the public enquiry into the development. The original plans for the redevelopment included a mammoth Arndale Centre that would have engulfed the area around Woolshops with a huge, enclosed H-shaped mall with five major stores and 49 smaller shops. Those plans even included the demolition of Piece Hall, which in 1972 had already been saved by a

single vote. Thankfully that idea was finally thrown out after a public inquiry in 1978, leading to the smaller 'open' scheme that now exists.

Demolition and building seemed to go on forever. Many will remember the bumpy 'temporary' car parks that existed for many years whilst councillors, planners and developers argued over how to rebuild. One of the few remaining buildings, the Sun public, house somehow survived the first phase of demolition, standing alone and forlorn in the emptiness until almost the last minute.

It was requested that many of the existing buildings be preserved. As a consequence the north parade of shops was rebuilt as close to the original structure as possible.

The crowning glory of the centre however, is the last remaining timbered building in Halifax town centre - No 3/5 Woolshops, now renumbered No 1. Commonly referred to as the 'Tudor' building, suggesting a date in the 16th century, it actually carries a datestone for 1670. Both are probably wrong; the official listing suggests it is 'probably early 17th century'. The colour of the woodwork (which imitates red lead) caused considerable controversy and many people still believe it is incorrect and should be black. English Heritage however, has said it is the correct colour.

The 1930s Prince's Arcade on the opposite side of the roadway was demolished along with an abattoir, leaving only the twin entrance towers to the arcade remaining.

As for the road itself between the shops, this was closed and made into today's pedestrian precinct. For the increasing numbers of shoppers who arrived driving their own vehicles a car park was constructed at the bottom of the street. Direct access car parking for over 300 vehicles would eventually be provided, with disabled spaces and free parking on Sundays and Bank Holidays.

Phase 1 of the Woolshops Shopping Centre opened in 1983. The development had cost £6.5 million. The first store to open was Boots the Chemist on Market Street.

Sainsburys was the original tenant of the premises which would subsequently be occupied by Marks & Spencer – now known as M&S. Sainsburys moved out to its new purpose-built superstore in the early 1990s. The empty unit was then refitted and Marks & Spencer opened in 1995.

Over the years shops have included high street names such as Dewhirst the

Butcher, Mister Minit, Currys, and Chelsea Girl (now River Island), along with smaller independent businesses such as Spinnies Café, and Earththings florist.

Phase 2 of the Woolshops development was completed in 2000, bringing with it Top Shop, Evans, Peacocks and Clinton Cards to Halifax. Superdrug and New Look also moved into larger units from elsewhere in the Centre.

Nor has the success of Woolshops been restricted just to its buildings. In 2007 Woolshops won a Gold Award from 'Yorkshire in Bloom'. The Woolshops received the accolade for Best in Category for Shopping Centres in Yorkshire and for Best Commercial Property. The Centre also received a special award for the most improved landscaping.

Judges comments included, "A well thought out design embraces spectacular vistas at the Woolshops."

Centre Manager, Jason Gregg, commented, "We are delighted that Woolshops has been recognised in this way. The award is a culmination of hard work between shopping centre staff and our partners at Calderdale Council".

Woolshops is currently managed by LaSalle Investment Management on behalf of the site's owner Coal Pension Properties.

Top left: Looking down Woolshops in the 1970s. *Below left: The first phase of building on the new Woolshops begins. Above and below:* Summer 1990 and the familiar view of a busy Woolshops*.*

'Sorry I'm late but a woman kept me talking'
The Nethercoats story

Today, the Halifax-based, specialised joinery company, Nethercoats, has grown into one of the region's pre-eminent designers and manufacturers of bespoke products used to create high quality working environments.

Though now a major local business, and founded more than half a century ago, the company is still proud to consider itself a 'family' firm.

Company founder, Eric Nethercoat, was born in Sheerness, Kent. War, however, brings with it many unexpected twists and turns to people's lives: during the Second World War, as a soldier Eric was stationed in Halifax. It was here that he met his wife, Pauline, and would eventually settle and raise a family.

Many people had a somewhat adventurous time during the war; and Eric more than most.

Involved in the invasion of Italy by the Allies, Eric was captured twice by the enemy. The first time he escaped, but was recaptured; the second time he got away by climbing up and over the rooftops of his prison. In the Italian countryside he found sanctuary with a local family who would become his life long friends.

Happily Eric survived his wartime adventures almost unscathed. However, due to the fact that he developed frostbite in his toes during his spell as a prisoner of war, on arrival back in England he was grounded. His only physical reminder of the war years was that thereafter he, understandably, remained extremely sensitive about people standing on his feet!

Though no longer fit for active service there was still war work to be done. Eric now went to work for the Ministry of Works. This stood him in good stead for his future career.

After the war Eric got a job with Mr Crossley of Spring Edge as a jobbing joiner undertaking every kind of task involving wood. Eric, however, being a Southerner,

often found it very difficult to make himself understood back in those days when 'foreign' accents were still a rarity, and many older Halifax folk still spoke broad Yorkshire. One day whilst doing a troughing job in King Cross, Eric asked the lady of the house for a 'pile'. She stared at him nonplussed and asked, "A pile of what?" Eventually the penny dropped. "Oh, you mean a bucket!" she said, and went inside the house to fetch the pail that Eric thought he had asked for.

Eric might have happily continued working for his employer for many years, but events now conspired to intervene. When his employer, committed suicide Eric decided that it was time to set up business on his own. Whilst his wife Pauline helped from an office at home in Emscote Avenue, Eric worked from the back of a handcart for a couple of years, with a small workshop at Hyde Park, doing odd jobs.

Those early post-war years were not easy. Many building materials, not least imported wood, were in short supply, and that which was available often went to large firms. Make do and mend was frequently the order of the day, with existing materials often recycled.

Despite the shortage of materials demand for household repairs and maintenance was high with many properties having been left for a long time without the necessary care as a result of so many men folk being away in the war leaving an enormous backlog of work to be done.

Cursed with a terrible memory Eric had an unfortunate habit of always being late. And when he did finally arrive he would always say, "Sorry I'm late but a woman kept me talking." This became a catchphrase amongst friends and family.

In 1952 the business moved to Dundas Street. By now Eric was employing two people. Pauline divided her time between the business and bringing up the couple's daughter and two sons. The dawn of the 'New Elizabethan Age' as 1952 was called was not only marked by the coronation of a

Far left: This photograph was sent to Pauline by Eric in July 1947. Left: A picture dating from a similar period to the one on its left, showing Eric and Pauline enjoying a day trip in Sheerness, Eric's home town. Above: Eric and Pauline at a celebration in the early 1970s.

to the World Cup at Wembley.

The optimism of those years knew no bounds. And in Halifax Eric Nethercoat expressed his confidence in the future by moving to new premises.

In 1966 the firm moved to Wakefield Road, Copley. Four years later Eric and Pauline's eldest son, Paul, joined the company as an apprentice.

The company now expanded. National economic growth continued and with it work for the firm. Not even the industrial unrest of the early 1970s and the famous 'three-day week' could dent the growing prosperity of Nethercoats.

Yet the future is unknown. In 1976 the company was hit with a terrible blow when its founder Eric Nethercoat died of a heart attack. After much heart-searching Pauline Nethercoat and David Harris decided to continued the business, and the firm became a limited company in 1977. David became Managing Director, Pauline became Chairperson and her son Paul now became foreman.

When David Harris semi-retired in 1996 Paul took over as

Above and below: Adam Iwanowski (top) and Chris Oldfield (below) at work insde Nethercoats' Brunswick works.

new, young Queen, but was also the start of an unprecedented era of prosperity for Britain. Few would have guessed it at the time but, as rationing ended, the remaining years of the decade would see living standards gradually rise to unheard of levels.

Such as yet unfulfilled promises of prosperity, however, were having little impact in Halifax. Not long after moving to Dundas Street in 1952 Eric went into partnership and moved to Bell Hall, remaining there for the next four years. The business, however, barely made enough to support Eric and Pauline, and it was with some regret that Eric ended the partnership and moved to Nichol Street, Spring Edge.

And now the promise of the New Elizabethan Age did begin to unfold. Soon Eric was employing six people. In 1959, two years after Prime Minister Harold Macmillan delivered his famous 'You've never had it so good' speech to the people of Britain, David Harris joined the company: he was later to become the firm's foreman.

With the arrival of the 'Swinging Sixties' it did indeed seem as if we had never had it so good: British music in the shape of the Beatles, and Rolling Stones along with many other British performers. The latest British fashions emanating from Carnaby Street were copied a round the globe. And in sport, glory of glories, England beat its great rival West Germany in a nail-biting final

Today the company's offices and workshop cover 25,000 square feet, with a team of over 60 skilled staff. The joinery and in-house polish shop have the very latest equipment, allowing the firm to combine the skills of its master joiners and craftsmen with the accuracy of digital woodworking technology.

From basic joinery, to complete bespoke office fit-outs, Nethercoats' skilled craftsmen bring interiors to life by project managing, manufacturing and installing quality bespoke items for discerning customers such as banks, building societies and major retail groups.

Managing Director, though with Pauline keeping a watchful eye on things.

Since 1996 under Paul Nethercoat, many changes have been made, mainly in the direction of manufacturing and installing specialised furniture, and projects using up-to-the-minute products, alongside traditional products.

As a result of expansion Paul promoted Jon Stanger to Managing Director to work alongside himself and his mother.

Pauline Nethercoat finally retired in 2006 at the age of 84 years (According to her son Paul, she had to be pushed into it!). Without her dedication and commitment over more than half a century the business would not have survived – perhaps it would never have even started.

Meanwhile, because of continuing expansion, conditions at Wakefield Road were becoming cramped. In January 2008 Nethercoats moved into Unit 16, Brunswick Industrial Estate, Westfield Street, Halifax.

Working with approved and nominated suppliers, sub-contractors and manufacturers, Nethercoats offers a full turnkey solution to all its clients who want the complete package with single point responsibility.

Nowadays, the company manufactures and fits quality specialised joinery for banks, building societies and major retail groups. Now employing 60 local people, all skilled in their field, Nethercoats looks to the future with confidence. With two generations of the family already actively involved with the business, it is hoped that the third generation will carry the company's expertise forward into the future.

Today, more than fifty years on from the founding of the firm, no one now ever says "Sorry I'm late but a woman kept me talking."

Above: *Paul Nethercoat (left) and Jon Stanger pictured alongside one of the company vehicles.* ***Below***: *Nethercoats Brunswick Industrial Estate premises.*

On The Road With R. Collett & Sons

R. Collett & Sons (Transport) Ltd is a family owned Company, established in Halifax over 40 years ago and with a history going back even further. Today the company specialises in General Haulage, Heavy Transport, Warehousing, Distribution and Handling.

The firm owns a modern fleet of over 40 vehicles and 70 trailers, which are fully maintained in-house on a purpose-designed 5-acre site, the Victoria Terminal, off Albert Road, Halifax.

Collett & Sons is one of Britain's leading specialists for moving heavy and abnormal loads. In particular it is the largest transporter of wind turbines in the country – an apt reminder of the firm's origins high in the Pennines.

The Collett story begins in 1928 when the first Richard Collett, known as Dick, started dairy farming at Hill Top Farm, Sutton, near Keighley.

Dick Collett was born in 1908 in Keighley. He was married with nine children, seven girls and two boys.

When taking his own milk to the dairy by horse and cart other local farmers asked Dick to take their milk to the dairy too. And so the R. Collett transport business began.

In 1933 the Milk Marketing Board (MMB) was established to market milk. Now instead of local farmers paying Dick Collett to take their milk to the local dairy the MMB paid for the collection of milk from the farms. On the strength of this Dick bought his first commercial vehicle.

That first wagon was a second-hand commercial vehicle bought for around £125 – a remarkable contrast with the company's latest wagon, a new MAN 250 ton heavy haulage tractor unit costing £140,000.

Above: Dick Collett with son Richard and daughters Irene and Sandra holidaying on the beach in Cleethorpes in 1947, the only holiday the family ever had. **Below left:** One of the early milk collection vehicles at Braithwaite Farm. **Below:** Richard Jnr pictured with Arthur Hutchinson, one of the first drivers for Dick Collett.

Richard Collett was born in 1942 in Keighley. He had minimal education due to his father needing him to work. Yet, Richard was not the type of person to let such a disadvantage hold him back in life.

A partnership between father Dick and son Richard was formed in 1964. As a result the firm now became R Collett and Son.

As well as the collection of milk, the partnership now started to carry animal feed for West Cumberland Farmers. As a result the business grew to 14 vehicles.

Over the following years the business grew from one wagon to seven. In 1939 Dick Collett moved from Hill Top Farm to Braithwaite Farm, Braithwaite, near Keighley.

The end of the Second World War in 1945 released ex-Army vehicles, chiefly Bedfords and Thorneycrofts to the commercial market and Dick Collett took advantage of the situation to expand the milk collection business.

Though the business may have been growing it was not an easy life. Milk had to be collected every single day of the year. Collecting from farms meant driving along the very worst of the area's country lanes and tracks. In winter they could be deep in snow — and the churns could be frozen to the ground. Diesel would freeze in the tanks, and if staff did not turn up for work then Dick himself would have to work both night and day.

In 1952 Dick Collett moved from Braithwaite Farm to the Station Hotel, Harecroft, Bradford. The next year, Hoyles of Halifax, a firm which collected milk from local farmers, left the milk business and the MMB asked Dick Collett if he would collect all the milk in the Halifax area. The milk was taken to the Halifax Dairies on Queens Road.

Billy Collett, Dick's eldest son, was part of the business of R. Collett. He left the business in 1956, however, when he moved to Brigg in Lincolnshire to farm. It was also at this time that the business took over Stubbs' garage at Cullingworth. The firm operated from these premises until 1959 when it moved to Back Lane Farm, Allerton, Bradford.

In 1959 Dick Collett also bought Buglers Transport, Todmorden, another milk haulier, and a further three vehicles were added to the fleet.

Dick Collett's younger son, the second Richard Collett, moved from Cullingworth to Moorfield Farm, Wainstalls, Halifax, in 1962. As a consequence the whole operation was shortly moved to that farm.

The business grew steadily, but in 1970 tankers took over from milk churns and the firm went into decline. Over the next three years, with farm collections falling drastically, the fleet of 14 vehicles shrank to just five.

And there was worse to come. In 1973 Dick Collett fell off the back of a vehicle whilst loading machinery at a woollen mill in Rishworth, above Ripponden, and tragically died as a result of his injuries.

Top left: A vintage milk collection vehicles on view at Collett's Victoria Terminal. Left: The company's first promotional material. Below: Richard Collett pictured in a tanker he purchased for Hebden Bridge chemical company, Aquaspersions Ltd, to help them in their expansion plans, 1983.

TAKE A LOAD OFF YOUR MIND!

THE LONG, THE SHORT AND THE TALL

COLLETTS
MOVE IT ALL

☆ Specialists in abnormal loads, crane hire and general haulage throughout the UK from 1 cwt to 125 tons.
☆ Urgent deliveries day or night.
☆ Regular service to London, South Wales, the Midlands, North East and Lancs.

NEED A LIFT?
CRANE HIRE SERVICE
To complement our already well established transport operation

FOR ALL ENQUIRIES RING NOW
244904 ☎ 244892
R. COLLETT AND SONS (TRANSPORT) LTD
MOORFIELD, WAINSTALLS, HALIFAX, HX2 7UQ

As the company grew, Moorfield Farm became unsuitable as an operating base, and in 1996 R. Collett and Sons (Transport) Ltd. moved to its current Halifax premises at Victoria Terminal, Albert Road, Pellon.

In 2008 the company bought a second depot at Goole to accommodate European business growth.

Investment continued in modern technology and equipment to enable the company to give its customers the very best service. State of the art computer systems link the Halifax operations with Goole.

However, though Dick Collett was gone the firm, continued. In 1974 the milk haulage side of the business was given up to concentrate solely on general haulage, and in 1975 the company of R. Collett and Sons Transport (Ltd) was formed.

The company continued to grow steadily but with Richard's five sons potentially coming into the business, more work had to be found. Although general haulage was successful and the business did grow, Richard realised that he needed a niche market and turned to heavy haulage.

Richard Collett the second's five sons did indeed eventually all join the business: Richard the third joined the company from school in 1976, his brother David in 1978, Lincoln in 1980 and Mark in 1981. Michael Collett went on to university, where he trained to be a chemist and went on to work for Allied Colloids in Bradford before joining the family firm in 1995.

Technical changes over the years also include advancement from the original rigid three ton wagon to 250 ton computerised, state

This page: Examples of the huge abnormal loads transported throughout the UK and Europe by Collett Heavy Transport.

of the art tractor units. Tracking devices for vehicles enable fast, efficient collections and deliveries for customers.

Similarly, the switch from rigid bodied vehicles to modular trailers means that today only the roads themselves limit what weight that can be transported along them. And R Collett & Sons have certainly carried some very large loads indeed.

The company's main market today is the energy and oil industry not least project-management of abnormal load delivery, such as wind farms, throughout the world. This includes not just road haulage and route surveys but also shipping and forwarding loads unsuitable to be moved by road by water transport, as well as heavy storage.

Today there are three generations of the Collett family in the business. Richard the second is Chairman and Chief Executive. His son, the third Richard Collett, is Fleet Engineer and Director. David Collett is Managing Director, Lincoln is Projects Director, Mark, Traffic Director and Michael Company Secretary and Director

In the next generation Richard Collett - the fourth of that name - joined the Company from school in 2000 as an apprentice auto engineer. He went onto study at Huddersfield College and won the top award of Apprentice Auto-mechanic of the year.

Jack Collett joined the company from school in 2007 as office junior and is now training to become a surveyor, planning safe routes for abnormal loads.

The company's winning business philosophy is succinct: it will arrange to move any load, any

quantity, large or small, normal or abnormal, anywhere in the world at a competitive price!

R Collett & Sons Ltd has grown from a farmer taking milk to the Keighley Co-op dairy with a horse and cart to become a successful international transport company operating by land, sea and air.

From just one member of staff in 1933, to ten in 1964, today the firm has 70 employees and is still growing. The financial situation has been transformed from a yearly turnover of hundreds of pounds to an annual turnover of millions of pounds. For the future the firm is committed to growth and expansion, acquiring other businesses that fit into the company's growth plan.

With yet another generation of the Collett family now growing up in the area, this remarkable family firm is set to still be delivering unusual loads far into the foreseeable future.

*Top left: One of Collett's fully articulated crane units. **Top right:** R. Collett & Sons (Transport) Ltd's Victoria Terminal, Albert Road, premises. **Centre:** A Collett Transport, Warehouse, Distribution flyer. **Below:** Collett's heavy transport team pictured in 2005 alongside a new TGA.*

Artisan Fireplaces - A Warm Welcome

According to the Ancients fire was first acquired by mortals when Prometheus stole it from the gods. Today, based at Phoenix Mill, Phoenix Street, Brighouse, Artisan Fireplaces Ltd promises a warm welcome to all its customers. This latter day successor to Prometheus is bringing light and heat to the folk of Calderdale, and far beyond.

Until the 16th century an open fire was the norm in most houses, with just a hole in the roof to let the smoke out. In the great houses of the 16th century, however, the fireplace was moved from a central position to an outside wall.

From then onwards a fine fireplace would be the focal point of British homes.

By the 1920s many homes were built with central heating, apparently negating the need for a fireplace. Yet despite central heating, fireplaces remain as popular as ever, and today every style and taste is catered for by Artisan Fireplaces.

Gary Heginbottom is a classic 'local lad'. Born in Halifax, Gary attended Sowerby Bridge Grammar School. A keen sportsman, Gary was playing rugby for the Old Crossleyans against Morley when he met the Morley Chairman who was also Chairman of Pawson's Stone Quarry in Morley; he offered Gary a job looking after the Pawson's Stone Fireplace showroom he intended to establish – and the chance to play rugby for Morley RUFC.

When Gary left school he worked in the fireplace showroom and played for both Morley RUFC and the England under-19s. Unfortunately Gary's rugby career was cut short by injury at the age of 21.

Gary now decided to set up his own business.

In 1986, with a bank loan, Gary and his then wife (and still good friend and business partner) Sue, established Artisan Fireplaces in Bradford Road, Cleckheaton.

A decade later the firm had shops in Cleckheaton, Bradford, Leeds, Wakefield and Huddersfield and had won the national title 'Fireplace Retailer of the Year'.

'Retailer of the Year' may have been fine, but Gary and Sue were even more ambitious.

Warehousing has been moved to Armytage Road, Brighouse, in order to offer even more showroom space and car parking for customers.

There is lift access to all three floors, toilets, and a coffee area in the main reception.

Now under one roof clients will find central heating and cool air experts, flue specialists, chimney sweeps, Corgi and Hetas installation advisers, all working alongside experienced Artisan Fireplaces staff.

Behind the Artisan sales force is a 10-van, 10-strong gas installation team, all Corgi registered, and directly employed by the company.

Today Artisan installs some 150 fireplaces every week for homeowners and builders alike, proudly boasting links with British Gas and major developers such as Britannia, Orion, Jones, Miller, David Wilson, Cala, Persimmon, Lovell and Circa.

Inevitably the large number of weekly installations creates a mountain of paperwork and Sue Heginbottom heads an administration team of 12 to cope with the finances, compliance procedures and legislation issues.

In 2007, after many overseas visits, Gary and Sue set out to become Britain's biggest fireplace retailer. They decided to bring all their five businesses under one roof in Brighouse to create not just the largest fireplace showroom in Britain but the largest in Europe.

The partners bought the largest premises they could afford, bringing all their experienced sales staff under one roof at Phoenix Mill. The new premises opened in March 2008, mirroring the successful 'centre of excellence' type of business common in Holland, Belgium and Germany.

Covering 30,000 square feet the showrooms display a staggering 500 fireplaces, over three floors, offering gas, electric and multi-fuel options as well as more than 50 working flue systems.

According to Sue 'We have invested heavily in premises and displays, but our main investment is in people – people who are proud to wear the Artisan logo, the same people Gary and I thank for reaching the levels we have now achieved.'

The company boasts an after sales service second to none, and has a strict no sub-contract policy. Staff turn up on the day agreed, on time every time.

Company turnover is now £4 million, and the aim is now to increase that to £7 million following the opening of a planned multi-fuel and stove centre.

Top, facing page: Gary and Sue Heginbottom. **Far left:** *The opening of Artisan Fireplaces in Bradford Road, Cleckheaton.* **Left, above and top:** *Interior and exterior views of Artisan's Phoenix Mill, Phoenix Street, Brighouse, fireplace showroom, the largest in Europe.* **Right:** *Gary and Sue with the team at Artisan, 2008.*

Rice-Jones - Help With The Law

Today's Rice-Jones, the well known firm of Halifax solicitors based in Westgate House, Market Street, is an amalgamation, dating from the early 1970s. Rice, Jones & Smith was established towards the end of the 19th century. Mr. Smith and Mr. Rice-Jones were joined by Mr Smith's son who succeeded to the practice in the 1920s. Mr J.E. Smith, the son, ran the business himself until 1962 when he took into partnership Mr. John Adshead.

Mr. Smith's business had been mainly commercial and he was involved in the flotation of many well known companies. He retired from the Halifax practice in 1967. Mr. Adshead was then joined by Mr. Grayham Smith.

The other half of the amalgamation, had its origins in the 1890s as a one man firm run by Sam Hoyle. When he retired, the practice was taken over by Herbert Boocock and the office was run by John Mackenzie, a managing clerk, who was then

joined by his son, Wallace when he qualified in 1929. When Herbert Boocock died in 1947, Wallace Mackenzie took over, practising in his own name. His son, Robert joined the business when he qualified in 1964. The firm then became Wallace Mackenzie and Son.

Those who are unfamiliar with the duties of a solicitor may imagine them to be routine and boring. But this is not so. Each case has its own interest and its own problems. Mr. Robert Mackenzie tells of a Halifax client who retired to Bournemouth and died, leaving an estate of £1.2 million to be disposed of. It was left to the children of the client's cousin and the deceased's only instruction was, 'You'll find them when the time comes.' Mr. Mackenzie saw a lot of hard work ahead, and the firm of Rice-Jones and Smith appealed to the Halifax Courier for help. As a result of the article that was published in the Courier Mr Mackenzie received a phone call from one of his client's old schoolfellows who had known all the people concerned. The legatees were all traced in a single afternoon!

Not every case is so easy to resolve however. Robert Mackenzie's father was not so lucky: Wallace Mackenzie had a client who had died a bachelor and had not made a will. His grandparents had been displaced persons in the First World War; and his mother had been one of nine children.

In this case tracing the legatees was very complicated. Eventually all 70 of them were rounded up. When the residue of the estate had been divided by that number, there was not a great deal for each of them to be thankful for. The moral of this story is - make a will!

The firm had been operating for a number of years from two sites within the town centre. In 1998 it was decided the future development of the firm and the quality of service given to clients would be best served if all the staff were under one roof. It was also decided to shorten the name to Rice-Jones.

Premises were found in Westgate House, a then recently-refurbished office block in the centre of town. The open plan accommodation was at that time very innovative for a High Street practice. The firm was now able to offer clients exactly the same high standard of professional advice and assistance, but in clean modern and comfortable surroundings benefiting from easy access for wheelchairs with lifts to the reception and interview rooms.

Over the years there have been a number of changes in the partnership, the current partners being Robert Mackenzie and David Hofton.

The firm also employs a number of highly qualified and specialised solicitors and legal executives together with support personnel. The firm has a Legal Aid franchise, and deals with a variety of work, including Personal Injury, Civil Litigation, Employment, Family, Child care and Matrimonial, as well as all aspects of residential and commercial conveyancing, Wills and advising the elderly, preservation of assets, tax planning, and probate in addition to Guardianship work, including Lasting Powers of Attorney and Receivership.

Servicing client's needs for over a century has shaped Rice-Jones into the firm it is today: dedicated, responsive, and in tune with local people's expectations.

*Top, facing page: Partners, Robert Mackenzie (left) and David Hofton. **Left:** A 1960s roof-top view of Commercial Street which shows Pearl House, the firm's former office being built. **Top left:** The modern legal practice which has a sympathetic approach to its clients. **Below:** Westgate House, home to Rice-Jones since 1998*

Finn Gledhill - Centuries of Service

Today the Halifax-based firm of solicitors, Finn Gledhill is one of West Yorkshire's major legal practices, providing a wide range of services to local, regional and national clients. Though the firm uses the very latest 21st century sophisticated Information Technology systems, its roots go back to three very old Halifax general practices.

The firm of Godfrey, Rhodes and Evans dates from the 1850s and traded from premises above the York County Savings Bank. FN Dickie was the last survivor of an even older firm, Frederick Walker Son and Dickie, established in the early 1900s as eventual successors of Robert Parker who practised in the 1700s and was also an MP for Halifax. Oaths are still taken today on a Bible bearing the name of Thomas Adams, one of Robert Parker's successors, and the date 1812.

Hugh Finn and Michael Gledhill began working together in 1960. From 1962 to 1965 they traded as Godfrey Rhodes and Evans. In 1965 on the death of Mr Dickie, they acquired the firm Fredrick Walker and Son and Dickie along with No 2 Harrison Road, still part of the present premises and moved there. At that stage they changed the name of the amalgamated firm to Finn Gledhill and Co.

As a result of that merger No 2 Harrison Road became too small to house the rapidly expanding firm, so a plan was considered to build a new four storey extension at the rear of No 2. In view of the estimated cost, the practice decided instead to purchase No 1 Harrison Road from Pickles the Architects. In 1969 Horsley, Bairstow and Helliwell, a firm established in the 1880s amalgamated with Finn Gledhill and Co. and No 3 Harrison Road was added.

The practice has grown rapidly since then. In 1962 it had consisted of just Hugh Finn and Michael Gledhill, together with one clerk and two secretaries. Today, there are 7 partners, 13 fee earners and 29 full and part time staff. The firm now occupies premises on both sides of Harrison Road. No 4 Harrison Road was acquired when the accountants, Whitham Smith Mitchell ceased to practice in the early 1980s. Finally No's 5 and 7 were acquired from insurance brokers in 1999.

Together these six properties form the firm's present headquarters in Halifax. There is also an office in Hebden Bridge following the acquisition of the law firm Eastwoods in 2002.

Today Finn Gledhill is recognised for being an up-to-date High Street practice where staff are friendly, approachable and welcoming, providing sound professional advice with value for

The Civil Litigation Department advises on all types of disputes from boundary disagreements to land law and tenant contractual disputes.

The Criminal Department boasts the only Halifax practice to have two solicitor advocates in the same firm, having earned 'higher rights' of audience, equal to those of barristers, which means they can represent clients in the higher courts, including the Court of Appeal and the House of Lords.

All Finn Gledhill's solicitors are experts in their particular fields. Solicitors dealing with probate and wills, for example, have completed an advanced probate course run by the Society of Trust and Estate Practitioners. In addition, the firm's senior family solicitor, who specialises in representing children and parents in care proceedings, has also earned "higher rights" of audience and is a member of the Association of Lawyers for Children.

Unusually, Finn Gledhill also boasts two Notaries, Michael Gledhill and David Lee. There are only four in the Halifax area. A Notary's job is to record facts under English Law. Notaries are appointed by the Archbishop of Canterbury. There are only about 1,000 in England and Wales.

By employing the very best people Finn Gledhill has been able to grow the practice whilst remaining local and continuing to offer the people of Calderdale a professional alternative to big city practices.

money, both for individuals and businesses. Finn Gledhill offer specialist legal advice in areas such as family law, relationship breakdown and separation, wills, probate, tax and residential conveyancing.

For businesses there is a dedicated Commercial Property and Business department which handles all types of commercial transactions including commercial disputes and supports local businesses and charities with advice and participation.

Finn Gledhill has its own independent financial adviser available for advice on capital investments, retirement and inheritance tax planning.

Far left, facing page: The origins of the three firms that amalgamated to form Finn Gledhill can be traced back to the 1700s. This line drawing of the North Bridge end of town, including the original stone bridge, shows the Halifax that existed at that time. **Top left:** *Finn Gledhill's No 2 Harrison Road, pictured in the 1990s.* **Left:** *The firm's No 1, No 3, No 5 and No 7 Harrison Road offices in 2008.*

Briggs Priestley - Signs of the Times

Briggs Priestley Ltd is an award-winning producer of signs and vinyl graphics, trophies and awards, screen and litho printing. It is one of Yorkshire's oldest engraving and etching companies.

The original Mr Briggs Priestley established the firm in 1893 as a small hand engravers at 22 Westgate, Halifax, just outside the Piece Hall gates. Still located in the heart of Halifax, though now based in Lord Street, the company today specialises in providing an extensive bespoke service to meet all its customers' requirements.

In the closing years of Queen Victoria's reign Briggs Priestley engraved cups and trophies for a living, as well as printing type, and designs in reverse, for litho printers and for chemical etchers.

In the early days brass, which was inexpensive and easily cut by the powerful Pantograph-designed engraving machines, was the material of choice. Acrylic or Perpsex would in time also become an important material after its first appearance in the 1930s. More than seventy years later it seems as if almost every material imaginable can now be printed on or etched – stainless steel, aluminium, wood, glass and plastic.

Briggs Priestley died in 1956 leaving the business to his family despite none of them being actively involved in it.

By then Arthur Armitage, father of the firm's present owner, had worked there for four years travelling daily from Leeds by tram.

Top: *An 1880s view of the Briggs Priestley's Lord Street premises which was then home to the Nags Head Inn.* ***Above:*** *The Nags Head was demolished in 1884 after it was bought by the corporation for road widening and replaced with these shops.*

Arthur approached Briggs Priestley's son-in-law, Selwyn Furness, then a cashier at Martin's Mill, with a proposition to buy into the business and continue the name of Briggs Priestley. Selwyn and Arthur now worked together. Selwyn Furness did the book keeping and dabbled in engraving, but it was Arthur who was the skilled craftsman and who in turn taught Colin Senior, the present foreman, as well as his son David Armitage, all about machine engraving.

Arthur's son David started full time work in 1963 the year after the firm moved from Westgate to 3 Lord Street. David had in fact previously worked in the business on Saturdays and Sunday mornings and during school holidays from the age of 11. David's younger brother Robert also joined the firm in 1968.

Sadly, Arthur Armitage passed away in 1971. However, an insurance payout enabled his sons David and Robert to buy out Selwyn Furness, so ending any involvement in the firm by its founder's family. Selwyn Furness now retired, left the brothers with exactly £200 in the bank, a sum which then equated to just one week's wages for the six staff.

Seven years later, in 1978, Robert Armitage decided to emigrate to Canada. His brother David now faced the challenge of finding the finance to buy Robert's half of the business or to sell up. Happily the Yorkshire Bank came up with the money. According to David Armitage 'It was well worth the risk. It only took me ten years to pay it back!'

Over the following years, with the help of long serving staff, the business was developed. David Woodhead set up the chemical etching side of the business, and Paul Hand, now a director, was instrumental in pushing the silkscreen department forward.

The firm expanded into 1 Lord Street and 42 Bull Green in 1995.

Today the company's own computerised graphics department under Dan Moss is responsible for all artwork and designs which enables the firm to produce etched plates, screen printing, and vinyl cut signs, graphics for vehicles and windows, brochures, cards and letterheads for the firm's own litho printing department

After more than a century in business the firm has built up an excellent reputation for its expertise, quality and value though the process used today were often not imagined even 50 years ago.

While the firm keeps well abreast of changing technology, it still produces some work using the old 'tried and tested' ways such as the repair or resilvering of cups and trophies.

Meanwhile, with its strong association with sporting events, Briggs Priestley tries to put something back into the community. It sponsors crown green bowling, cricket, rugby and football, as well as many other sports.

From its beginnings in the 19th century to the 21st century Briggs Priestley has embraced the best technology of each period, ensuring that the firm's name has always been, and remains, the 'sign of the times'.

Top left and above: *Example of bespoke signs, etchings and vinyl graphics produced by Briggs Priestley Limited.* ***Below:*** *Owner David Armitage outside Briggs Priestley's Lord Street premises, 2008.*

Joseph Dobson & Sons - Sweet Success

The Calder Valley has long had a reputation as a centre for sweet-making. One of the longest-lived names in the business is that of Elland-based Joseph Dobson & Sons Ltd established in 1850. With some 25 members of staff, the business still operates from its original premises in Northgate Elland. The factory and office premises are set around a cobbled courtyard.

A passageway leads into the courtyard from Northgate where it is still possible for visitors to see the grooves cut into the stone flags to give horses a better grip when pulling the delivery carts.

Born in the late 1820s, Joseph Dobson was orphaned as a child after his parents died during an outbreak of the plague. He was raised by his grandparents in York, where for a time he worked for the confectioners Cravens of York. Joseph married Eleanor Berry (who was the sister of William Charles Berry whose family were the joint founders of Terry's chocolate factory at the turn of the century).

Joseph and Eleanor moved from York to Elland in 1850 to claim Joseph's inheritance. On arrival in Elland, however, they found that only some land and buildings remained: the local solicitor

acting as trustee had disappeared with all the money due to Joseph. Despite that setback, undaunted and without any capital, Joseph and Eleanor started their own confectionery firm producing 'Bride Cakes' and 'Funeral Biscuits' which were popular during Victorian times.

Gradually sweets were introduced, one of the most popular being 'Conversation Lozenges' which were mild herbal tablets flavoured with rose, violet or vanilla and inscribed with mottoes such as 'Take ye not to strong drink' and 'Always speak the truth'.

Joseph and Eleanor had seven children. After Joseph's death his three sons, Robert, William and Thomas, took over the business.

In 1930 Thomas John Dobson, the youngest of the three sons, was managing the business. It was he, we believe, who invented the famous 'Yorkshire Mixtures' after slipping down the factory steps whilst carrying some trays of boiled sweets. When he saw the assortment on the floor the idea of 'Yorkshire Mixtures' immediately occurred to him. These continue to be one of Dobson's best selling

This is the Original Wrapper of Joseph Dobson, founder of the Firm of Joseph Dobson & Sons, Limited. Date of Printing, 1852.

FROM J. DOBSON, GENERAL CONFECTIONER, Northgate, ELLAND.

Bride Cakes and Funeral Biscuits and all kinds of Confectionery to order on the shortest notice, and on the most reasonable terms.

Top left: *Founder Joseph Dobson.* **Above:** *Dobson's first wrapper dating from 1852.* **Centre:** *Early tins of Humbugs and Yorkshire Mixtures.* **Below left and below:** *Sweet making, pouring the mixture and sweet and die pressing.*

PURITY & QUALITY

lines, and contain 18 different varieties of sweets.

During the Second World War Dobson's was allowed to purchase only a proportion of the raw materials it had used before the war. However, the varieties that could be made were not reduced. Ration coupons were issued to customers, who were only allowed to purchase a small quantity of sweets each month. In 1949 when rationing ended there was such a rush to buy that rationing had to be reintroduced for two more years.

The raw materials, cane sugar, glucose and water, have not changed over the years, and Dobson's continues to make products by boiling these ingredients together in open pans. Once the mixture has reached the required temperature it is poured on to large slabs where the other ingredients are added and mixed by hand. As the mixture cools it is fed through rollers which is how the many shapes and sizes are formed. This is the same traditional method used by previous generations.

Today the most popular sweets include Yorkshire mixtures, voice tablets, mint imperials, pear drops, and bonfire toffee. Particularly popular with children are Rainbow Crystals and Sherbet Pips. In 1999 Dobson's bought local lollipop company, Ryburn, and now manufacture 15 varieties of lollies alongside the original Dobson's products. The most popular lollies are Traffic Light, Tutti Frutti, Tropical Fruit and Cola.

Today the company is managed by the fifth generation of the founding family. Miriam Walshaw (Joseph Dobson's great-great

granddaughter), and her husband Stephen, joined the business in 1999 after moving from Canada with their two daughters Josephine and Charlotte.

Dobson's sweets are available throughout the country through several supermarket chains. In addition Dobson's also supplies many wholesalers and independent shops. Dobson's is also entering the e-commerce market, offering a large selection of confectionary products for sale over the internet.

Proud of their heritage, Dobson's also offer factory tours for organised groups of sixteen persons or more. The public can get a fascinating insight, by way of demonstrations, of the traditional skills of the confectioners and see how the same techniques have been modernised in the interests of safety and hygiene.

Whilst meeting all the challenges of a 21st century marketplace, happily Dobson's still maintains all the old-fashioned tastes and traditions of the 19th and 20th centuries.

Top and above right: Early 20th century pricing and product labels. Above left: An early 20th century picture of the Dobsons shop. Far left: Edwin Dobson, son of John Thomas Dobson. Bottom left: Modern day pouring of the boiled sweet mixture from copper pans on to slabs. Left and below: Owners Miriam and Stephen Walshaw at work. Miriam is pictured in the shop with a selection of Dobson's famous sweets whilst Stephen checks on the Mint Imperials.

RP Dowsland - The Age of Electricity

The firm of RP Dowsland Electricians Ltd was established in 1955 by, not surprisingly, Mr RP Dowsland. He had previously worked in electrical engineering for MF Farrar of Crossley Street, Halifax.

Following the retirement of Mr Farrar, Mr Dowsland started his own business at Wesley Court, Crossley Street, which, being directly opposite the Town Hall steps, was a prime location. The company employed many electricians and apprentices through the years. Mrs Dowsland managed the shop and carried out the office work.

Starting the business in the mid-1950s was perfect timing. Although Halifax had a good supply of electricity the age of electronics had not quite arrived. Older residents could still recall the days before Halifax had electricity. All that had changed with an electric grid being installed to power the first trams.

Yet even by the 1950s, half a century later, there were still many homes in Halifax that were wholly reliant on gas. In the outlying rural areas many homes would not get electricity until the 1960s.

Gaslights were the norm on our streets. In our homes there were few electrical appliances but lights, kettles, vacuum cleaners and toasters were relatively commonplace. But as yet few homes could boast other luxuries such as washing machines, fridges and televisions.

Yet the second half of the 1950s would transform Britain. The austerity of the immediate post war years would give way to a period of unprecedented prosperity. As Prime Minister Harold Macmillan would famously say we'd 'never had it so good'.

Above: One of the company's earliest vehicles, a Ford Thames van with Mr Dowsland at its side. **Left and below:** *1960s views of the shop on Wesley Court.*

And with that sudden, unexpected, prosperity came an equally unprecedented demand for electricity and electrical goods.

Wind-up gramophones and accumulator-powered wirelesses may have been good enough before the war, but now folk wanted radiograms which played the new 45 and 33 1/3 rpm records. They wanted televisions on which to watch not only the BBC but also ITV, that brash new channel with adverts.

Consumer goods which had been in short supply for years now began to appear in the shops. The latest in washing machines, fridges and freezers, food mixers and electric cookers were now affordable by most. And for those who couldn't afford to pay cash there was another novelty: hire purchase – the new 'buy now pay later' option which fuelled even greater demand.

Truly there was never a more auspicious time to start a business dealing with anything involving electricity.

Michael Hartley joined the company in 1976 as an electrician and continued to work there as an employee until February, 1988, when the business founder Mr Dowsland retired, handing the firm over to Mike. Mrs Dowsland continued to work, showing Mike's wife, Beverley Hartley, her job.

After Mike and Beverly Hartley took over the firm and Mr and Mrs Dowsland had both fully retired the Hartley's

daughter Leanne joined them. Leanne became part of the team on leaving school and came to work in the shop and office whilst going on day release to college to learn typing, administration and computer skills. Leanne is now a key person in the administration of the company.

In 2001 Adam Hartley, Michael and Beverly's son joined the firm as an apprentice electrician. A few years later he successfully completed his apprenticeship.

Over the years the firm steadily expanded and bought another workshop in Blackwall, moving some of its contracting work there.

After a poor few years of retail trade in the original shop it was decided to close that side of the business in order to move with the ever-changing demand of the electrical industry. In 2005 the shop where the enterprise began was closed and Dowsland's moved out to its workshop at 20A Blackwall, enabling the firm to keep up with the times whilst still continuing to give the kind of personal service expected from a true family firm.

Though the field of electrics has changed immensely over the decades traditional values never do. Dowsland's still endeavours to offer all its customers every courtesy and care.

The business still offers the same values as it has for over 50 years: quality, customer care and expertise. It is those qualities that made Dowsland's into a well-respected name within the local community, qualities which will no doubt see it through its second fifty years.

Top left: Mr Dowsland inside the shop in the 1960s.
Below: The Hartley family: Beverly, Mike, Leanne and Adam outside the company's Blackwall premises.

Southdale Homes - Homes to Be Proud Of

'Homes fit for heroes' was a Government slogan of the 1930s. That promise to the soldiers, sailors and airmen who had fought in the Great War of 1914-18 was however, a long time being fulfilled.

Another world war stopped the house-building programme of the 1930s dead in its tracks. And even after that war ended in 1945 shortages and rationing of building materials ensured that the plans for slum clearances and new building, which had been promised a generation earlier, would have to wait until the 1960s and 70s to come to fruition. In truth it would take almost half a century of relative austerity for Britain's home-building industry to regain the confidence and optimism which had so characterised the late Victorian era, the period when so many of the homes and buildings familiar to Halifax residents were built.

Not until Prime Minister Margaret Thatcher's government reinvigorated the national economy in the 1980s would Britain be able to fully enjoy a boom sufficiently sustainable to kick-start a building industry long in the doldrums. And in West Yorkshire two men knew an opportunity when they saw one.

Southdale Homes is part of the Southdale Group. Based in Halifax, they have been building quality homes throughout the North of England since the 1980s.

The company was founded in 1988 by Chris Harris and John O'Hara. Their first development was Prospect Mill, Skircoat Green, Halifax and it was after this, and a couple of other small developments, that in 1991 they bought their first office premises at Haley Hill, Boothtown.

Although the partners started their business in a very difficult trading period, they quickly developed a formula for success by securing work with housing associations. As the business continued to expand in the late 1990s, the decision was made to purchase new office premises on Clare Road, Halifax.

By this time Southdale had completed a wide variety of developments ranging from new housing, a children's home, refurbishment of a church and works to ageing council stock. The firm quickly outgrew the premises on Clare Road. The search began for new offices which eventually led to the old Butler and Asquith Engineering Works, on Westholme Road, where Southdale is based today.

*Top: Where it all began, the company's original premises in Haley Hill, Boothtown. **Below left:** The site of Southdale Homes' first project; Prospect Mill. **Below:** In 2005 a prestigious gold award was presented to Southdale Homes in what is regarded as the Oscars of the House Building Industry; The Daily Telegraph "What House?" Awards. Pictured from left to right are: Noreen Beck, Housing Manager for Kirklees Neighbourhood Housing, Mike Atherton OBE and Paul Moore,*

Southdale Homes is now one of the region's largest social housing developers, with expertise in the development of mixed-tenure communities, providing low cost housing for rent and sale for its development partners. The company's knowledge of area regeneration has helped to create revitalised and sustainable communities in otherwise blighted areas.

Southdale's sister company, Circa, is its private division specialising in new homes for sale. It specialises in building stylish, yet practical homes for the private market in the Yorkshire, Lancashire and North East areas. Circa has developed a new portfolio of house designs to suit the contemporary living styles of their target market and launched these at their first development in 2005.

Circa's first development, Serenity, was in Copley, on a site just behind Copley cricket club. A huge success, it has been a springboard for other developments including Topshelf at Buttershaw, Chequers and Quattro at the Deighton and Brackenhall initiative in Huddersfield, Inspired in Blackburn, and '4 U 2 View' in Barnsley. Due to the rapid success of Circa since its creation, and the growth in staff numbers to help facilitate this, Southdale and Circa were outgrowing their shared office space at Westholme Road.

In July 2007 a decision was made to move Circa to its own premises leaving Southdale to expand further across the Westholme Road office area. Circa's offices are now on Gas Works Lane, in Elland, right on the canal, opposite the rear of the Barge and Barrell pub.

On a day-to-day basis, Southdale Homes is now run by Managing Director Paul Moore, and Circa is run by Managing Director Chris Harris - one of the original partners in the company. The other founding partner, John O'Hara, retired in early 2008.

Southdale Homes' turnover as a division last year was £26 million, but combined with Circa, Southdale Group's turnover exceeded a remarkable £47 million.

Through heroic enterprise those 'homes for heroes' have finally arrived.

Above: Field Hurst, the company's first executive house development. Below: Circa's new offices on the canal in Elland.

McVitie's Cake Company - At The Cutting Edge

The McVitie's Cake Company's Kingston Mill factory in Hopwood Lane began life long ago as Riley's sweet factory. The Riley brothers started the business in their own house before moving to Hopwood Lane in 1911.

The site has seen many changes over the years. One employee who has lived through it all is Enid Croad. She joined the business as a bright-eyed 15-year-old in 1962. Her first job was office junior. In those days the site was still a sweet factory, making products like Nuttall's Mintoes and Chocolate Toffee Rolls. Office work was completely different with no computers, manual typewriters and mechanical adding machines that had big crank handles. For the payroll all employees had clocking in cards that had holes punched in them when entering and leaving the site – with payroll using the holes to calculate the wages.

The business remained independent for over fifty years before it was purchased by the Guinness group, which sold out later to Callard and Bowser.

In 1988 came the sale of Callard and Bowser to United Biscuits, and with it the factory. United Biscuits had been founded in 1948 following the merger of two Scottish family businesses — McVitie & Price and MacFarlane Lang.
McVitie's has a strong cake-baking heritage. McVitie's has been making royal wedding cakes since 1893 when McVitie's and Price made one of the wedding cakes for King George V and Queen Mary. The cake was so well received that a tradition grew for McVitie's and Price to supply future royal wedding and christening cakes. The two tier cake was made with the finest ingredients, coated in marzipan and sugar paste and decorated with a range of hand crafted edible decorations. The design has been carefully developed to include a blend of elements used in the original cake and also from the present day. The cake was displayed on the original solid silver stand and formed part of a private family celebration at Clarence House.

Around 1940, cake production had been set up at the company's factory in Harlesden, London, to take advantage of the distribution benefits afforded by the Grand Union Canal. In 1947, McVitie and Price made the official wedding cake for Princess Elizabeth and Lt. Philip Mountbatten. The top tier of the wedding cake was saved for the christening of Prince Charles on 15 December, 1948.

Top: *Early 20th century view inside the Riley factory.*
Below: *A horse-drawn car with 'Another Load of Rileys Toffee'.*

because there was room for expansion, but, more importantly, because the Managing Director of the Cake Company was so impressed by its fine production record despite far from modern equipment.

The 300-strong staff of 1973 had by then been whittled to 150, but the changes immediately necessitated 60 new jobs with the expectation of many more. McVitie's invested £5 million, and the site became the management centre for United Biscuits' expanding cake business.

By the 1960s it was the aim of United Biscuits' company Chairman, Sir Hector Laing, to make McVitie's the lowest cost producer of bar cakes. He achieved this, helped by the high-tech automation at Harlesden, where

production was centralised during the 1970s, alongside the biscuit factory. Business at that time focused on long-life products, such as bar cakes, fruitcake and traditional Christmas cakes, and benefited from shared distribution costs with the biscuit factory.

New opportunities came in the 1980s. Better transport facilities and a move away from home-baking towards a more convenient lifestyle resulted in increased business for McVitie's Cake Company and increased profits. To capitalise on this, the Cake Company was set up in 1989 as an independent business unit, with its own dedicated management team. This development brought with it an increased focus on innovation, leading to the launch of Jamaica Ginger, Golden Syrup, Jaffa and Penguin cake bars. The individually wrapped cake bar sector, pioneered by McVitie's, remains even now the fastest growing sector in the total cake market.

The unprecedented success of these new products meant that a new manufacturing facility had to be established, and so production moved to Halifax. Not only did the move mean a significant reduction in overhead costs, but also the situation of Halifax near to the M1, M62 and M6 offered obvious benefits for distribution. The factory in Hopwood Lane was chosen partly

In 2004 a new production line was commissioned to produce flapjacks, although the capacity of the line has since increased to produce cake slices and other types of snack bars. In manufacturing terms the line is state of the art and employs such things as hi-tech sonic knives, putting McVitie's quite literally at the cutting edge of cake manufacturing.

In 2007, in keeping with its long traditions, the firm made the official celebration anniversary cake for the 60th wedding anniversary of HM The Queen and HRH Duke of Edinburgh in addition to cake slices given to the Royal Household.

Top left: A 1920s view of the packaging department. Above left: 'By Jove look who's ere'; Rileys Toffee takes pride of place in a confectionery shop window. Below: A 2008 interior view of the Hopwood Lane factory.

Nestlé - Where Quality Counts

In 1890, Violet Mackintosh opened a home made cake shop in King Cross Lane in Halifax. She was a good baker and the little venture prospered. Her husband, John, meanwhile was foreman in a silk mill. However, he was a partner in his wife's business and continually invented new lines to add to the range of scones, tea cakes and parkin. She experimented with sweet making and managed to produce a toffee that was different.

Working at nights, the couple produced just a few batches of the toffee to sell on Saturdays only. A few days prior to the introduction of this new venture, John put a bill in the shop window. "Mackintosh's Celebrated Toffee. Come and eat at our expense!" He understood his fellow Yorkshiremen!

The following week another bill told them they had tasted at the shop's expense and now they would have to taste at their own. Soon Violet could no longer cope with the demand when she had cakes to bake as well. John decided to give up his mill work and join her in the toffee business. They produced more of it than could be sold in the shop, so John went 'on the road' to other small shops in Halifax, He borrowed £50 for a horse and cart, though he hated debt. Some of the Mackintosh relatives were brought into the business and, in spite of some temporary setbacks, they all prospered. A move was made from King Cross Lane to a small rented factory. By 1898, he had managed to put aside £11,000. He needed to borrow a further £4,000 to build his own factory in Queens Road and his first priority was to pay off this debt. Sales spread throughout Yorkshire, then throughout the UK.

From the very beginning, John Mackintosh put aside a small percentage of the takings for advertising. When the North Pole was reached for the first time, Mackintosh's poster showed a tin of toffees in the snow there with a caption that read, 'If you can't get Mackintosh's toffee in your neighbourhood, leave the neighbourhood!'

Leaving relatives to produce and sell at home, John travelled, looking for new markets. As early as 1902, he had factories in the USA and Germany. In 1908, he was joined by his eldest son, Harold, but in 1914 the two eldest boys volunteered to defend their country, Harold in the navy and Douglas in the army, despite Douglas being under-age. John spent the time preparing to extend the business when the war finished. However, it was not to be. John died suddenly, at the early age of 51, in 1920, within a year of his sons rejoining him.

When the Queens Road factory burnt down in November 1911, the company moved to Albion Mills immediately. Queens Road was rebuilt as a chocolate factory and Harold Mackintosh was sent to Germany to learn chocolate making. A.J. Caley in Norwich was taken over in 1932 and John's third son, Eric, was sent there as managing director. Harold Mackintosh was chairman from 1921 until his death in November, 1964.

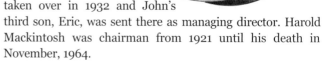

Top left: *John Mackintosh, founder of the company at his desk with his eldest son - later to become Viscount Mackintosh.* **Left:** *The Mackintosh's Sand competition in August 1922. The picture (made in sand) was a reproduction of ML Attwell's picture 'The Fairies' toffee town.* **Above:** *On Friday March 20th 1931 the Daily Dispatch carried this advertisement for Mackintosh's Carnival Assortment. 'You can pick and choose to your palate's content' customers were told.*

In 1969 John Mackintosh and Sons Ltd. merged with Rowntree to become Rowntree Mackintosh. Less than 20 years later it was announced that the company would change its name to Rowntree plc with effect from 30 June, 1987. The new name was not destined to last long as the following April Jacob Suchard launched the dawn raid that saw share prices soar. However, it was the old Swiss firm that won in the end, and in 1988 Rowntree plc was bought by Nestlé.

The Halifax site currently employs around 600 people operating 24 hours a day, 7 days a week, producing Quality Street, Easter Eggs and Walnut Whips. The Hazelnut in Caramel sweet is the most popular in the Quality Street assortment, but every sweet is somebody's favourite.

Mackintosh's was one of the first firms in England to set up a health service for their employees. It benefited the management too, since skin diseases are dangerous in a food factory and bad teeth do not help hygiene. There was no NHS and most employees did have skin and teeth problems. One shilling a week bought health care, including dentistry, at the firm's expense.

Nestlé Confectionery (UK) is now a far cry from the little shop opened by the formidable lady in her deeply fringed shawl. After her death in 1932 a parcel was found labelled 'Never to be opened'. Of course her surviving relatives did open it. Inside they found Violet and John's marriage certificate, Violet's certificate as a Sunday School teacher and the original toffee recipe. The little collection represented the principles on which she based her life - Family, Faith and Work.

The Mackintosh range of confectionery was boosted in 1935 with the launch of Rolo, joined a year later in 1936 by Quality Street, which gained its name from J.M. Barrie's play. Chocolate and toffee were used together for the first time in Quality Street, which, at that time was said to be an expensive product, priced at sixpence a quarter pound.

When forty five shillings was the average factory wage, it would take two hours to earn enough to buy one pound. Nowadays, at about £3 for a pound, it would take only about forty minutes.

On 8 June, 1941 the firm's 50th anniversary was celebrated. Because the date John Mackintosh's business was established was uncertain, he chose the date of the birth of his first son, so that the company celebration coincided with Harold's 50th birthday. Harold was presented with a book signed by every employee.

By the 1960s, Harold Mackintosh had been made a Viscount and Douglas and Eric were joint managing directors of the firm. Douglas's sons, Peter and Martin, joined the business as development engineer and chartered accountant respectively.

Top left: A delivery wagon dating from the 1930s. *Left: A wartime advertisement.* *Right: What's your favourite? Quality Street, a people's favourite since 1936.* *Below: A view inside the factory today.*

Suma - Fair Prices for Fine Food

Suma is an unusual enterprise, a worker co-operative in which the worker members own and manage the business. The business is well-known within the green, ethical and alternative communities. Suma canteen veggie lunches are amongst the most sought after anywhere. And according to Suma staff "We eat what we practice!"

A wholesaler and distributor of wholefoods and vegetarian foods, and green household products, many products are made locally, like its Calder valley-sourced Suma soaps and beers.

The co-operative was founded by seven friends in Leeds in 1977 as Triangle Wholefoods Collective Ltd. but soon became known as Suma.

In 1986, the co-operative moved to Halifax's Dean Clough, by which time it had 30 members. Ernest Hall welcomed Suma as his first big tenant, into the old Axminster shed - remembered by many Halifax people in its Crossley's carpets days.

Suma survived a catastrophic flood in 1989 when the warehouse filled up with dirty water and hundreds of tons of spoiled food had to be destroyed.

Despite that setback Suma once again outgrew its premises. With most of the members being locals, the next move had to be close. Fortunately in 2001, thanks to Marshalls, Suma obtained one of the new distribution centres on the Lowfields industrial estate in Elland.

Suma now has 110 worker members and £25 million annual sales. Customers are throughout the UK and exports go as far as Hong Kong and the Falkland Islands.

Committed to ethical business, Suma supplies many fair-trade foods and products which ensure a fair return for farmers and producers.

Suma is also very green – buying renewable electricity and working hard to cut its carbon footprint. Each year to soak up the emissions from their delivery lorries, and to reduce flooding from the runoff of deforested hillsides, Suma members plant thousands of trees in the Calder Valley with local charity Treesponsibility.

Anyone who would like a talk about healthy wholefoods, green business, co-operatives or starting a food co-op is invited to contact info@suma.coop

Top left: Suma members outside the company's Dean Clough premises in 1988. Below: A group photograph to celebrate Suma's thirtieth anniversary.

Hartley & Sugden - Still On The Boil

For over 140 years, Hartley & Sugden Ltd has been manufacturing hot water boilers in Halifax. Many famous product names have come from the company's Atlas Boiler Works in Gibbet Street, including the 'White Rose' cast iron sectional boiler and 'SCP' mild steel hot water boiler. Coal fired boiler plant and the Compact steam boiler are a speciality for the company, with many innovative designs being produced over the years.

The business began in 1867 as a partnership between Zaccheus Sugden and Colonel John Edward Hartley. They had joined forces in order to take over from the executors of a boiler-making business which had been started in Halifax by the recently deceased S T Crook.

Hartley was a well-known local figure, a Colonel in the Militia, who used to ride to his office on a white horse. Sugden by contrast was of humble origins and much less is known about him

In the 1860s boilers were made of wrought iron plate which had to be fabricated into complicated shapes and sealed by a process known as fire-welding: both edges were heated in a blacksmith's hearth until white hot and then hammered together.

Soon after the partners took over cast iron began to replace wrought iron, a new foundry was established in Albert Road from where castings were delivered to the firm's Atlas and Premier Works by horse and cart.

Today, Hartley & Sugden market one of the most comprehensive ranges of high-efficiency industrial and commercial boilers available in the United Kingdom. Most fuels are catered for and outputs range from 40 kW to 6000 kW. Boilers are manufactured in cast iron and steel.

Over the years Hartley & Sugden have been suppliers to Governments, Local Authorities, Hospital Trusts and major commercial organisations. Overseas markets are mainly in the Middle East, China and Hong Kong, Africa and Europe.

In the last 70 years the company has changed ownership a number of times. Today the firm is owned by Ormandy Ltd, a major force in the construction and supply of package plantrooms and heating solutions, mainly for large projects such as hospitals and commercial buildings.

*Top left: J E Hartley, former Managing Director of Hartley & Sugden, 1913. **Above:** A view of Altlas Works around the turn of the last century. **Left:** Patent for White Rose Magazine Fuel Feeder Sectional Boiler. **Below:** A boiler about to leave Hartley & Sugden for delivery to its destination.*

BIRD'S EYE VIEW

When Ewan MacColl composed 'Dirty old town' for a scene in his 1949 play 'Landscape with chimneys', he was thinking of Salford. The description of the song, that has been recorded by such diverse acts as The Spinners and Rod Stewart, could have been applied to most industrial scenes pictured in the last century. Halifax was just one of many skylines dominated by the smoking stacks from the 'dark, satanic mills' to which William Blake alluded in 1800. The cooling towers and mill chimneys belched poisonous gases into the air above the town and mixed with the smoke rising from domestic hearths to leave a pallor of murk and mist that was a permanent feature of the environment in which we once lived. The industries provided us with our livelihood, but considerably shortened the three score years and ten in which we could enjoy the fruits of our labour. Respiratory diseases abounded and it was a common sight, especially in late autumn and early winter, to see people on their way to work or school spluttering into hankies and face masks that were meant to protect them from the dirt and grime that was everywhere. The decline of the mills and a raft of air quality legislation in the 1950s improved things considerably, but for many it was a cough or two too late.

Aerial photography became very popular in the interwar years. It provided a new way of looking at our towns and their layout that would help planners get a better feel for future projects in that they did not have to visualise everything from ground level on a two dimensional plan. New roads and housing could be better designed with the assistance of photographs such as this one in 1931. Looking west over Elland it shows the little town to be a compact mix of housing and mills. Many of the latter have now gone, or have been converted into flats or given over to other uses, but here we can see evidence of the large number of mills that once flourished there. Elland, referred to as 'Elant' in the Domesday Book, was more important than its neighbours Halifax and Huddersfield in the Middle Ages and a major centre for wool production. The modern spelling comes from the Lord of the Manor, John de Eland, who was granted a charter by Edward II to hold markets and fairs on his land. Elland Hall, the family mansion, stood in the vicinity of Calderdale Way, the link road to the M62. Its remains were completely removed in 1978. In addition to wool, the town was also well known for the durable flagstones that it produced and the Calder and Hebble Navigation provided a useful method of transportation to the rest of the county. Elland was also home to the Gannex raincoat firm founded by Joseph Kagan just after the Second World War.

Seen from the southeast, the 1931 aerial view of West Vale looks towards the River Calder at the top of the picture. The open land of the sports ground on the river's south bank is just as it was, though augmented by a nursery along the eastern side of the land. A walk through the woods around Clay House is still a pleasant experience and the 17th century building is a most attractive Jacobean piece of architecture well worth a visit. The terraced garden makes a delightful backdrop for wedding party photographs. Moving south, across Rochdale Road, Greetland Cricket and Bowling Club continues to offer an exercise opportunity for lovers of willow and lignum vitae. The large mill, hemmed in between the railway viaduct, Saddleworth Road and Stainland Road now houses Andy Thornton's architectural antiques. West Vale School is in the centre of the photograph and most of the housing we can see is still with us today and has been complemented by further housebuilding after World War II. Barkisland is to the west of the photograph and Elland to the east.

Below: This vista across Savile Park towards Wainhouse Tower was taken from the hillside at Exley in 1966. Exactly a century earlier, Captain Henry Savile of Rufford Abbey sold Skircoat Moor, then valued at about £40,000, to Halifax Corporation for the nominal sum of £100, on condition the corporation took action to alleviate smoke pollution in the town. In recognition of his generosity, the moor was renamed Savile Park. The name 'Skircoat' is thought to mean 'buildings of rocks' and may well have referred to the early stone built houses that were erected on the edge of what became the village green. Some wags used to call the place 'Furcoat' as many of the elegant houses in the vicinity of Savile Park can only be afforded by those with more than a few bob in their pockets. Historically, freeholders had been able to graze their livestock on the moor, so they were thankful to Captain Savile as this could continue. Even after such practices diminished and disappeared with time, the land has remained sacrosanct and is a delightfully large green oasis close to the town centre. At the top of the picture, in front of Wainhouse Tower, we can see Crossley Heath School, a former orphanage and with links back to Tudor times through its Heath Grammar School connection.

Above: It was in 1966 that this panorama was captured from the dizzy heights of the top of the first Halifax Building Society office block. To all soccer lovers that means only one thing: England won the World Cup. It is very easy to recall that date as it is the only occasion in history that the national side has won anything. European tournaments come and World Cups go, but never so much as a glimmer comes our way. For those who prefer loud music, the Rolling Stones were blasting out 'Paint it Black' and the Troggs telling us what it was like 'With a Girl Like You'. It was still just an era when going to the cinema was popular, but bingo and the counter attractions of television had more than made their mark as major competitors. The ABC, in the centre of the scene, was showing a most unremarkable double feature of 'The Idol' and 'The Skull'. The former was a stupefyingly boring sex drama starring Jennifer Jones, who should have known better having once won an Oscar playing St Bernadette. The latter a Peter Cushing horror movie to silly to describe. This Wards End cinema began life as the Regal in 1938 before changing its name in 1961. It was later called the Cannon, reverting to the name ABC just before closing and eventually becoming Jumpin Jaks nightclub.

This aerial photograph dates from 1973, a period of change in many towns, including Halifax. Burdock Way, towards the top of the scene, was completed, thus relieving some of the congestion in the town centre. This was the culmination of the plans for a by-pass first mooted in 1947. Alderman John Burdock, chairman of the Highways Committee at that time, was awarded the OBE in 1971, partly for his work inspiring this project. A year after the road opened saw a major political change for the incumbents of the Town Hall, near the centre of the photograph. Local government reorganisation throughout the country meant the redrawing of borders and the re-allocation of powers. Even some counties disappeared off the map. Small towns, such as Elland, Brighouse, Ripponden, Sowerby Bridge, Hebden Bridge and Todmorden lost their independence and were swallowed up into something called Calderdale. These little places felt robbed of their independence and, even today, many resent being ruled from Halifax, seeing it as some sort of plot hatched just off Crossley Street.

Left: The bird's eye view along Sowerby Bridge's Wharf Street indicates the route towards the junction with Wakefield Road to the upper right, where the Prospect Veterinary Centre now stands. Above here the road forks around Pye Nest and Crow Wood Park. The right hand side of the town is still dominated by the mills and warehouses that were once the cornerstones of its prosperity. In the 19th century, there were extensive cotton, worsted and corn mills, large wharfs, several chemical works, iron foundries and a gas works. However, the five major mills were all closed by 1984 and the other industries had long gone. A quarter of the town's shops closed in the 1970s and early 1980s. Sowerby Bridge needed the equivalent of a blood transfusion to survive as its core industrial use had gone. Fortunately, a regeneration programme was begun almost immediately. The redundant mill buildings and warehouses were remodelled to provide housing, a canoe club, workshops, retail units, offices, a hotel, restaurants, a museum and visitor centre. Carlton Mill, one of the town's most formidable buildings, was transformed and has become a regeneration flagship. If only the powers that be can now do something about the vehicle log jam and the seemingly countless number of traffic lights that contribute to the slowest half mile journey in Calderdale.

Above: In 1970, the Sowerby Bridge Station dominated the top of Station Road. The sweeping approach, passing the handsome viaduct on the left, gave an imposing view of this fine building. It dated from 5 October, 1840, when it was opened by the Manchester and Leeds Railway Company. It served the community well for over a century but, following a disastrous fire in October, 1978, it was lost to the town and was eventually demolished in 1980. Its replacement was built in 1981, though not on the same site. The police station roof, on the corner of Norland Road, can be seen towards the bottom of the picture. Built in the 1930s, it was formerly the Labour Exchange. The boys in blue moved in after spells at the Town Hall and the Gothic style purpose-built station that is now a doctor's surgery. The railway line that swings away towards the top of the photograph is heading for Halifax, with a journey towards Luddenden Foot, Todmorden and, eventually, Manchester for those travelling in the opposite direction. A branch line to Ripponden and Rishworth once ran west from here, but that closed in the late 1950s as the mills in the villages began to be phased out. The road to the left of the viaduct leads towards the council tip and is a favourite with car drivers dodging Sowerby Bridge's infamous rush hour jams as it is possible to get out onto Wakefield Road via a narrow bridge.

Burdock Way was nearing completion in 1973, as seen from this bird's eye view. It now casts a shadow over North Bridge that nowadays has relatively light, local traffic. A previous bridge was opened in 1774 to assist journeys along the turnpikes that ran to Bradford through Queensbury, in one direction, and via Wibsey in the other. A replacement bridge was completed in 1871. It was designed by John Fraser and the building costs were remarkably low for the time, coming in at just £21,000, which was a modest amount for such a large enterprise. The two arches each have a span of 160 feet and the height of 16 feet carried the road well above the railway, allowing locomotives to travel underneath with ease. The tall central section contains a time capsule in which coins, newspapers, photographs and other artefacts were lodged. A statue commemorating the life and work of Edward Akroyd was erected on its southwest corner in 1876, but this was moved 25 years later to near All Souls' Church. The first road bridge in this vicinity that carried traffic across the valley was a small single arched stone one, but this collapsed in 1770.